The ESSENTIALS® of

Psychology I

Linda Leal, Ph.D.

Associate Professor, Department of Psychology
Eastern Illinois University–Charleston, Illinois

> This book covers the usual course outline of Psychology I. For additional topics, see *"THE ESSENTIALS OF PSYCHOLOGY II."*

Research & Education Association
61 Ethel Road West
Piscataway, New Jersey 08854

THE ESSENTIALS®
OF PSYCHOLOGY I

Year 2004 Printing

Printed in the United States of America

Library of Congress Control Number 99-76839

International Standard Book Number 0-87891-930-9

III-4

WHAT "THE ESSENTIALS" WILL DO FOR YOU

This book is a review and study guide. It is comprehensive and it is concise.

It helps in preparing for exams and in doing homework, and remains a handy reference source at all times.

It condenses the vast amount of detail characteristic of the subject matter and summarizes the **essentials** of the field.

It will thus save hours of study and preparation time.

The book provides quick access to the important definitions, principles, practices, and theories of the field.

Materials needed for exams can be reviewed in summary form— eliminating the need to read and re-read many pages of textbook and class notes. The summaries will even tend to bring detail to mind that had been previously read or noted.

This "ESSENTIALS" book has been prepared by an expert in the field, and has been carefully reviewed to ensure accuracy and maximum usefulness.

Dr. Max Fogiel
Program Director

Contents

CHAPTER 1

Introduction to Psychology

1.1 Defining Psychology and Psychologists

Psychology is the study of behavior. Psychologists study both human and animal behavior as well as **overt** (external and observable) and **covert** (internal and nonobservable) behaviors.

The **goals of psychology** are to
(1) describe behavior,
(2) predict behavior,
(3) explain behavior, and
(4) control behavior.

Psychologists have either doctoral or master's-level degrees. A **doctoral degree** (Ph.D., Psy.D., or Ed.D.) is received after three to six years of post-undergraduate training in psychology. A **master's degree** (M.S. or M.A.) is granted after one to three years of post-undergraduate training in psychology. Some areas of psychological training at both the doctoral and master's degree levels require an additional year of **internship** or on-the-job training in a clinic, hospital, school, or business setting.

1.2 Major Subfields of Psychology Today

While in graduate school, psychologists are trained and specialize in one major subfield of psychology.

The majority of psychologists are either **Clinical** or **Counseling**

1

Psychologists, who study the causes, treatments, and diagnoses of behavioral, emotional, and mental health problems.

Cognitive Psychologists study internal thinking, such as the processing of information, memory, and concept formation.

Comparative Psychologists study and compare behaviors across different species of animals, including humans.

Developmental Psychologists study age-related changes in behavior from the prenatal period through old age. (Some examples include the study of how memory, language, or cognitive behaviors change with age.)

Educational Psychologists work on school-related issues such as designing curricula, teaching, or counseling methods that can be used in the schools.

Experimental Psychologists rely on scientific methods to conduct research in such areas as learning, memory, and sensation and perception.

Industrial or Organizational Psychologists generally work in business or industry on such problems as optimum working conditions, selecting employees, and marketing products.

School Psychologists work directly with students, teachers, or parents in the school setting. School psychologists test, counsel, and make recommendations about individual students who are referred because of learning, emotional, or behavioral concerns.

Social Psychologists study all aspects of social behavior and how people interact with other people. For instance, they study aggressive behavior, helping behavior, friendship formation, etc.

1.3 Historical Approaches to the Study of Psychology

Wilhelm Wundt (1832-1920) began the first experimental psychology laboratory in 1879 at the University of Leipzig, Germany. This occurred as a result of the merger of **philosophy** (questioning truth) and **physiology** (scientific analysis of living organisms). Wundt studied **introspection,** the careful analysis of one's own conscious experiences. Since 1879 there have been several historical approaches to the study of psychology:

2

Historical Approach (Associated names)	Description
Structuralism Edward Titchener (English, 1867-1927)	Examined the structure of the mind, analyzed structure and content of mental states by introspection, and was concerned with reducing experience to its basic parts.
Functionalism William James (American, 1842-1910)	Proposed the study of how the mind adapts us to our environment. Influenced by Charles Darwin's theories of evolution and natural selection. Felt conscious experience is adaptive and always changing.
Behaviorism Ivan Pavlov (Russian, 1849-1936) John B. Watson (American, 1878-1958) B. F. Skinner (American, 1904-1990)	Stressed the study of observable behavior, not unobservable consciousness.
Psychoanalysis Sigmund Freud (Austrian, 1856-1939)	Emphasized the study of unconscious mental processes; argued that people are driven by sexual urges and that most emotional conflicts date back to early childhood experiences.
Gestalt Max Wertheimer (German, 1880-1943)	Emphasized perception and that stimuli are perceived as whole entities rather than parts put together ("The whole may be greater than the sum of its parts.")
Humanistic Carl Rogers (American, 1902-1987) Abraham Maslow (American, 1908-1970)	Stressed that humans have enormous potential for personal growth. Emphasized importance of free will, the human ability to make choices, and the uniqueness of the individual.
Cognitive Jean Piaget (Swiss, 1896-1980)	Studied internal, mental representations that are used in perceiving, remembering, thinking, and understanding.

1.4 Research Methods

Psychological research is based on the scientific method. The **scientific method** consists of
- (1) defining a research problem,
- (2) proposing a hypothesis and making predictions,
- (3) designing and conducting a research study,
- (4) analyzing the data, and
- (5) communicating the results and building theories of behavior.

A **sample** is a subset of a population selected to participate in the study. All of the participants in a research study make up the sample.

A **population** includes all members of a class or set from which a smaller sample may be drawn and about whom the researcher wants to draw conclusions.

A **random sample** is one in which every member of the population being studied has an equal chance of being picked for inclusion in the study.

A **biased sample** occurs when every member of a population does not have an equal chance of being chosen.

A **stratified sample** is one in which every relevant subgroup of the population is randomly selected in proportion to its size.

A **subject** is an individual who is actually participating in the research study.

Replications refer to research studies that are repeated, often under different conditions, in order to ensure the reliability of the results.

1.4.1 The Experiment

Psychologists use experiments to determine **cause-and-effect relationships**. An **experiment** requires that the researcher systematically manipulate or control one or more variables and then observe how the research subjects or participants respond to this manipulation. The variable that is manipulated is called the **independent variable**. The response that is measured after the manipulation of the independent variable is known as the **dependent variable**.

An experiment consists of at least two groups of subjects. The **experimental group** is the group that is exposed to the manipulation of the independent variable. Some experiments have more than one experimental group, meaning there are several manipulations of the independent variable. The **control group** of an experiment is not exposed to manipulation of the independent variable. The responses of subjects in the control group are compared to the responses of subjects in the experimental group(s) in order to determine if the independent variable(s) had any effect on the dependent variable.

Subjects usually are assigned to groups in an experiment based on **random assignment** that ensures that each participant had an equal chance of being assigned to any one of the groups. Random assignment helps guarantee that the groups were similar to one another with respect to important characteristics before the manipulation of the independent variable. When subjects are not randomly assigned to groups, it is referred to as a **quasi-experiment**.

Subject bias occurs when research participants' behavior changes because they know they are being studied or because of their expectations. A **placebo** is an inactive substance given in the place of a drug in psychological research. A **placebo effect** occurs when participants believe they are experiencing a change due to an administered drug which is really a placebo. **Observer** or **researcher bias** occurs when the expectations of the researcher influence what is recorded or measured. **Double-blind technique** is used to control for both subject and observer biases. In the double-blind technique, neither the subjects nor the researcher who is measuring the dependent variable knows who is assigned to which group in an experiment.

A **single-subject experiment** involves the participation of only one subject. The independent variable is systematically changed over time, and the subject's behavior at one time is compared with the same subject's behavior at another time. In this case, time is used as the control.

1.4.2 Nonexperimental Methods

Nonexperimental methods of research do not include the systematic manipulation of variables by the researcher and thus cannot be used to discuss cause-and-effect relationships.

Correlational research involves measuring two (or more) variables in order to determine if they are related. If the value of one variable increases in value as the other also increases in value, this is known as a **positive correlation**. A **negative correlation** occurs when there is an inverse relationship between the variables measured; as the value of one increases, the value of the other decreases.

A **correlation coefficient** is a number that represents the strength of the relationship between the variables measured. A correlation coefficient can range in value from 0 to 1. A **correlation coefficient of 0** indicates no relationship between the variables measured. A **correlation coefficient of 1** indicates a perfect relationship between the two variables: you can predict one variable perfectly by knowing the value of the other. Therefore, the closer a correlation coefficient is to 1, the stronger the relationship between the variables measured, and the closer a correlation coefficient is to 0, the weaker the relationship. Even if a strong correlational relationship is found, however, cause-and-effect conclusions *cannot* be made because there was no systematic manipulation by the researcher.

Naturalistic observation is a research method that occurs in a natural setting that has not been manipulated by the researcher. The researcher systematically observes and records what occurs in an unobtrusive manner. This is done so that the behavior of the subjects being tested is not altered. **Interobserver reliability** is the amount of agreement between two (or more) observers who simultaneously observe the same event.

A **case study** is an in-depth study of a single subject. It can include interviews, observations, and test results.

The **survey method** of collecting data requires the researcher to ask a group of people about behaviors, thoughts, or opinions. Data is collected through questionnaires or interviews.

1.4.3 Comparing Research Methods

Method	Strengths	Weaknesses
Experiment	Can make cause-and-effect relationships. Researcher has control.	Sampling errors. Often hard to generalize to real world.
Correlation	Can study real world behavior. Can determine relationships.	Cannot determine cause and effect.
Naturalistic Observation	Can gather information in its usual setting as it naturally occurs.	Cannot determine cause and effect. Observer bias possible.
Case Study	Intensive information can be gathered about individuals.	Cannot determine cause-and-effect. Expensive and time consuming. May not be able to generalize information gathered to others. Biased sample possible.
Survey	Large amounts of information can be gathered from many people in a relatively short period of time.	Cannot determine cause and effect. Biased sample possible. Response bias possible. Survey questions might not be reliable or valid.

1.4.4 Ethical Guidelines

The **American Psychological Association (APA)** has published ethical guidelines to follow when conducting psychological research with human subjects. Some important points from these guidelines include:
- Psychologists are responsible for the ethical conduct of research conducted by them or by others under their supervision.

- Psychologists conduct research with due concern for the dignity and welfare of the participants.

- Psychologists inform participants that they are free to participate or to decline to participate or to withdraw from the research at any time.

- Psychologists inform participants of significant factors that may be expected to influence their willingness to participate.

- Psychologists must obtain informed consent from research participants prior to filming or recording them.

- Participants should be fully debriefed following any deception.

- Psychologists inform research participants of their anticipated sharing or further use of personally identifiable research data.

- Psychologists provide a prompt opportunity for participants to obtain appropriate information about the nature, results, and conclusions of the research.

- Psychologists must honor all commitments made to research participants.

- The APA also presents additional guidelines for the **use and care of animals** in research.

CHAPTER 2

Biological Basis of Behavior

2.1 The Nervous System

Functions of the nervous system:
(1) Processes incoming information,
(2) Integrates incoming information,
(3) Influences and directs reactions to incoming information.

2.1.1 Divisions of the Nervous System

The nervous system is divided into the **central nervous system** and the **peripheral nervous system:**

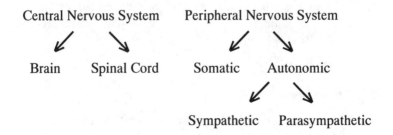

All nerves encased in bone make up the **central nervous system.** The central nervous system is responsible for processing information and directing actions.

9

The **peripheral nervous system** is made up of all nerves that are not encased in bone, and its main function is to carry messages to and from the central nervous system.

The **somatic division** of the peripheral nervous system carries messages inward to the central nervous system from the sensory organs (by means of **afferent** or **sensory neurons**) and outward from the central nervous system (by means of **efferent** or **motor neurons**) to the muscles for action. A **reflex arc** occurs when an afferent message travels to the spinal cord and an efferent message for action immediately returns to the muscle, bypassing the brain.

The **autonomic division** of the peripheral nervous system is responsible for involuntary functions of the body. This autonomic nervous system is divided into the **sympathetic** (known as the "fight or flight" branch; activates the body for emergencies) and **parasympathetic** (quiets the body and conserves energy) **branches:**

Sympathetic Branch	Parasympathetic Branch
Dilates pupils	Constricts pupils
Inhibits tears	Stimulates tears
Inhibits salivation	Increases salivation
Activates sweat glands	Decreases heart rate
Increases heart rate	Constricts blood vessels
Increases respiration	Decreases respiration
Inhibits digestion	Stimulates digestion
Releases adrenaline	Contracts bladder
Stimulates glucose release	Stimulates elimination
Relaxes bladder	Stimulates sexual arousal
Inhibits elimination	
Inhibits genitals	

2.1.2 Neurons

Neurons are specialized cells that transmit information from one part of the body to another. **Nerves** are bundles of neurons. The **function** of most neurons is to **receive information** from other neurons and to **pass this information on.**

Structural features of neurons:

Soma — The **cell body** of the neuron.

Dendrites — The branching projections of neurons that **receive information** from other neurons and conduct information **toward** the **cell body**.

Axon — The long, thin fiber that **transmits information away from** the cell body of a neuron **toward other neurons**.

Myelin Sheath — An **insulating material** that **encases** some axons and permits **faster transmission** of information. **Prevents** neurons from **communicating randomly**.

Synapse — The small **space** between neurons where communication takes place.

Terminal Buttons — **Small knobs** at the end of axons that **secrete chemicals**.

Synaptic Cleft — A **microscopic gap** between the terminal button of one neuron and the cell membrane of another. The place where chemicals are released.

2.1.3 Communication within the Nervous System

The nervous system is considered an **electrochemical system**. Communication within a neuron is **electrical**; communication between neurons is **chemical**.

Neurons are filled with and surrounded by electrically charged molecules called **ions**. A neuron at rest has an ion distribution that makes the axon more negatively charged than the outside of the nerve cell. **Resting potential** is the stable, negative charge of an inactive neuron and is the term used to describe the difference in electrical potential between the outside and the inside of a resting nerve cell. Under these conditions the soma and axon are said to be **polarized**. The brief change in electrical charge that is caused by a dendrite being stimulated or **depolarized** and by the resultant inflow of positively charged sodium ions is called an **action potential**. A **spike** is a nerve impulse generated by the neuron reaching action potential. After the firing of an action potential comes the **refractory period** when no further action potentials can fire.

The firing of a neuron or action potential is an **all or none propo-**

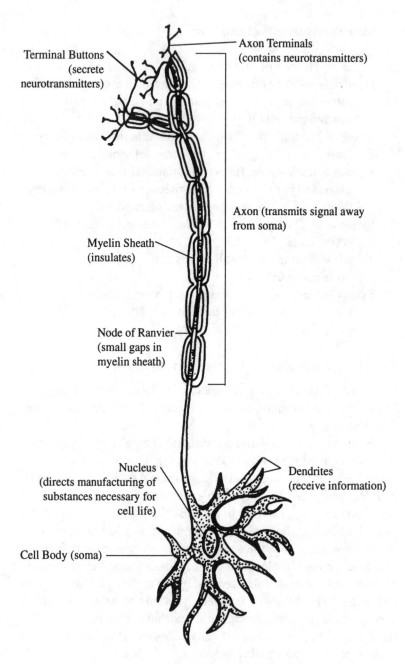

Terminal Buttons
(secrete
neurotransmitters)

Axon Terminals
(contains neurotransmitters)

Axon (transmits signal away
from soma)

Myelin Sheath
(insulates)

Node of Ranvier
(small gaps in
myelin sheath)

Nucleus
(directs manufacturing of
substances necessary for
cell life)

Dendrites
(receive information)

Cell Body (soma)

Figure 2.1: A Typical Nerve Cell

sition. This means that the neuron will fire an action potential of a high magnitude independent of the size of the original stimulus. In other words, if there is no stimulus, there will be no action potential. If there is a stimulus, weak or strong, there will be an action potential.

A neuron passes its message on to another neuron by releasing chemical **neurotransmitters** into the synapse. A **presynaptic neuron** sends the neural message and a **postsynaptic neuron** receives the message. A neurotransmitter can stimulate a postsynaptic neuron only at specific **receptor sites** on its dendrites and soma. Receptor sites respond to only one type of neurotransmitter. This **lock and key model** means that specific neurotransmitters work only at specific kinds of synapses. Neurons that respond to the same neurotransmitter form a **neurotransmitter system**.

Neurotransmitters may **excite** or **inhibit** the next neuron. Stimulation of an **excitatory synapse** makes the neuron more likely to respond; stimulation of an **inhibitory synapse** makes production of an action potential less likely.

Examples of neurotransmitters include:

Neurotransmitter (Abbreviation)	Function	Associated Disorders
Acetylcholine (ACh)	Excitatory neurotransmitter related to movement of all muscles as well as arousal, attention, anger, aggression, sexuality and thirst.	Memory loss in Alzheimer's Disease.
Dopamine (DA)	Inhibitory neurotransmitter that controls posture and movement.	Parkinson's Disease; Schizophrenia
Gama-aminobutyric acid (GABA)	Inhibits central nervous system and regulates anxiety and movement.	Anxiety disorders; Huntington's Disease

Neurotrans-mitter (Abbreviation)	Function	Associated Disorders
Glutamate (Glu)	Major excitatory neurons in central nervous system; important for learning and memory.	Memory loss; Alzheimer's Disease.
Norepinephrine (NE)	Important for psychological arousal, mood changes, sleep, and learning.	Bipolar mood disorder
Serotonin (5-HT)	Regulates sleep, mood, appetite, and pain.	Depression

Antagonists are drugs that inhibit neurotransmission. **Agonists** are drugs that stimulate neurotransmission.

Endorphins and **neuromodulators** are chemicals that act at the synapse of neurons. Endorphins are **neuropeptides** (made from **amino acids**) and occur naturally in the brain. They decrease a person's sensitivity to pain. **Neuromodulators** do not carry neural messages directly, instead they can either increase or decrease the activity of specific neurotransmitters.

2.2 The Brain

Gray matter refers to the neurons in the brain **without myelin**. **White matter** in the brain consists of **myelinated neurons**.

The **cerebral cortex** is the outer surface of the brain. It contains fissures called **sulci** and convolutions called **gyri**. The cerebral cortex processes all perceptions and complex thoughts. In evolutionary terms, it is the most recently developed brain structure.

The brain can be monitored using certain devices:
PET scanning (positron emission tomography) creates a visual image of functioning in various parts of the brain by tracing chemical activity.
MRI (magnetic-resonance imaging) scanner is another imag-

14

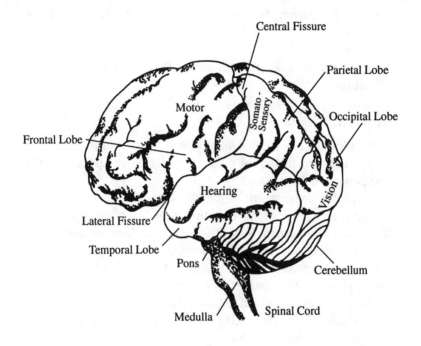

Figure 2.2: Major Areas of the Brain

ing technique that provides clear pictures of the structural anatomy and chemistry of the brain by passing a strong magnetic field through the person's head.

CAT scan (computerized axial tomography) presents a picture of the human brain by passing X-ray beams through the head at various angles.

EEG (electroencephalograph) records the electrical activity of the brain.

The brain can be divided into the **hindbrain,** the **midbrain,** and the **forebrain.**

2.2.1 The Hindbrain

The **hindbrain** is located in the bottom portion of the brain and is an extension of the spinal cord. In evolutionary terms, it is the oldest portion of the brain.

The **major components of the hindbrain** are:

Medulla — The oblong structure at the top of the spinal cord that controls many vital life-support functions such as breathing, heart rate, and blood pressure.

Pons — Located above the medulla. Connects the lower brain regions with higher brain regions. Also helps regulate sensory information and facial expressions.

Cerebellum — Located at the rear of the brain and controls movement, coordination, balance, muscle tone, and learning motor skills.

Reticular Activating System (lower) — Monitors the general level of activity in the hindbrain and maintains a state of arousal. Essential for the regulation of sleep and wakefulness. Sometimes referred to as the **reticular formation.**

2.2.2 The Midbrain

The **midbrain** continues upward from the pons portion of the hindbrain and lies between the hindbrain and the forebrain.

The midbrain **relays sensory information** from the spinal cord to the forebrain.

The **upper portion** of the **reticular activating system** is located in the midbrain.

2.2.3 The Forebrain

Not only does the **forebrain** make up the largest part of the brain, it is also the most highly developed portion of the brain.

The **major components of the forebrain** are the following:

Cerebrum — The largest part of the forebrain; is responsible for complex mental activities. Its outer surface is the **cerebral cortex** and is divided into two **cerebral hemispheres**. Contains four major lobes: the **frontal lobe** that controls voluntary movement and includes the **motor cortex**; the **parietal lobe** that contains the primary **somatosensory area** that manages skin senses; the **occipital lobe** is located in the back of the head and contains the **visual cortex**; and the **temporal lobe** contains the **auditory cortex** and is located on each side of the head above the temples.

Limbic System — Related structures that control emotion, motivation, and memory. Contains **amygdala** and **hippocampus**.

Corpus Callosum — Enormous communication network that connects the right and left cerebral hemispheres.

Thalamus — Relays and translates information from all of the senses, except smell, to higher levels in the brain.

Hypothalamus — Plays a major role in the regulation of basic biological drives and controls autonomic functions such as hunger, thirst, and body temperature. Regulates the **pituitary gland**.

2.2.4 Hemispheres of the Brain

The cerebrum is divided into two hemispheres known as the **right** and **left cerebral hemispheres**. The main interconnection between the two hemispheres of the brain is a large set of axons called the **corpus callosum**.

Severe **epilepsy** may be treated by cutting the corpus callosum which results in a **split brain**.

The left hemisphere controls the right side of the body and the right hemisphere controls the left side of the body.

Although both hemispheres are capable of carrying out most tasks, the left hemisphere is often more active in verbal and logical tasks and the right hemisphere usually specializes in spatial, artistic, and musical tasks.

2.3 Hormones and the Endocrine System

The **endocrine system** is a system of glands that release chemical messengers called **hormones** which are carried by the bloodstream to target organs.

Major glands of the endocrine system:

Gland	Hormones Secreted	Description
Adrenal Cortex	Steroids	Regulates salt and carbohydrate metabolism.
Adrenal Medulla	Adrenaline Noradrenaline	Prepares body for action.
Gonads	Estrogen Progesterone Testosterone	Affects reproductive organs, sexual behavior, and physical development.
Hypothalamus	Neurosecretions	Controls the pituitary gland.
Pancreas	Insulin Glucagon	Regulates sugar metabolism.
Pituitary Gland	Thyrotropin Oxytocin Corticotrophin Prolactin	**Master gland;** controls growth and other glands.
Thyroid Gland	Thyroxine Calcitonin	Regulates metabolism.

CHAPTER 3

Sensation

3.1 Psychophysics

Psychologists study the senses because we come to know our world primarily through them and what we sense often affects our behavior. Our senses inform us of the **presence of stimuli** or of any **change in a stimulus.** The first experimental psychological techniques were developed for the study of sensation. These techniques were called **psychophysical methods.**

Psychophysics is an area of psychology that examines the relationship between sensory stimuli and individual psychological reactions to these stimuli. Psychophysics has been traditionally concerned with detecting thresholds. The smallest amount of a stimulus that can be detected or noticed at least 50 percent of the time is called the **absolute threshold. Difference threshold** or **just noticeable difference (jnd)** measures how much a stimulus must change before it becomes noticeably different.

The study of just noticeable difference thresholds lead to **Weber's Law** which states that the amount of change needed to produce a jnd is a **constant proportion** of the original stimulus intensity. Weber's Law indicated that the more intense the stimulus, the more the stimulus intensity has to be increased before a change is noticed. For example, if music was being played softly, a small increase in sound would be noticeable. If the music was being played loudly, it would require a much greater increase in sound to perceive a difference in volume. Stated mathematically, Weber's Law asserts:

$$\frac{\Delta I}{I} = C$$

where

$$\Delta I = \text{jnd}$$
$$I = \text{stimulus of intensity } I$$
$$C = \text{a constant}$$

Fechner generalized Weber's finding to a broader relationship between sensory and physical intensity. **Fechner's Law** states that constant increases in a sensation produce smaller increases in perceived magnitude:

$$S = k \log I$$

This equation asserts that the magnitude of **sensation, S,** increases in proportion to the **logarithm (log)** of **stimulus intensity, I.**

Signal detection theory is a mathematical model that states that individual expectations, prior knowledge, and response bias influence the probability that a stimulus will be recognized. Signal detection theory does not deal with the concept of thresholds but deals only with varying **probabilities** that a stimulus will be **detected.** It takes into account the willingness of people to guess by determining the probability of a person guessing that there is a stimulus or **signal** present when there actually is one and the probability of a person guessing that there is a signal when there is not one. The person's response will depend on the **criterion** she or he sets for how certain she/he must feel before responding "yes, I detect it."

3.2 Vision

The sense of vision is sometimes referred to as our most essential or our **dominant sense.**

3.2.1 Light

Light is the physical stimulus for vision. The **visual spectrum**

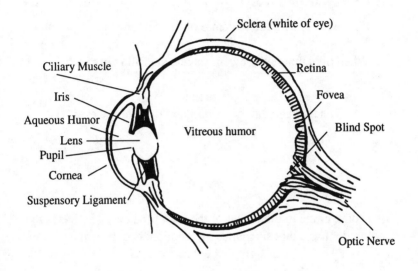

Figure 3.1: Structure of the Human Eye

(light that is visible to the human eye) is made up of various wavelengths of light measured in **nanometers (nm)**. A nanometer is one-billionth of a meter, and the visual spectrum varies from 400 nm to about 700 nm. Wavelength determines **color**, and the **amplitude** or height of the wave determines **brightness.**

3.2.2 Structure of the Eye

Figure 3.1 shows the structure of the human eye.

When light enters the eye, it travels the following path:

Cornea

The transparent outer bulge in front of the eye.

Pupil

The dark circle in the center of the iris of the eye. The **iris** is the colored muscle that surrounds the pupil and controls the amount of light that enters the eye.

Lens

Focuses light onto the retina. **Accommodation** occurs when the curvature of the lens adjusts to alter visual focus — the lens **flattens** for **distant** objects and **fattens** for **close** objects.

Retina

Converts light into impulses that can be transmitted by neurons to the brain.

After light passes through the cornea, pupil, and lens of the eye, it goes through the **vitreous humor** until it reaches the retina. The **retina consists of** several layers of cells, including:

Cones — Photoreceptors that are responsible for color vision and visual acuity. They are concentrated in the central region of the retina, the **fovea.**

Rods — Photoreceptors that are responsible for vision in dim light, peripheral vision, and black-and-white vision. Their density is greatest just outside the fovea, and then gradually decreases toward the periphery of the retina.

Bipolar Cells — Cells through which a visual stimulus passes after going through the rods/cones and before going to the ganglion cells.

Ganglion Cells — The axons of the ganglion cells form the **optic nerve.** The optic nerve carries the visual message to the **occipital lobe** of the brain for interpretation.

Other features of the retina include:

Fovea — Tiny spot in the center of the retina that contains only cones. Visual acuity is greatest at this spot.

Blindspot — Location where optic nerve leaves retina; contains no rods or cones. You cannot see anything that reaches this part of your retina.

Horizontal Cells — Retinal cells that connect rods with other rods and cones with other cones. Appear responsible for **Opponent-Process Theory** of color vision (see page 27).

Amacrine Cells — Large retinal neurons that connect ganglion cells laterally. The functions of most amacrine cells are unknown.

3.2.3 Eye to Brain Pathways

The path that visual information travels from the eye to the brain is shown in Figure 3.2. Visual information from the right side of the visual field for each eye exits from the left optic nerve of each eye and meets at the **optic chiasma,** where it is combined and sent to the left side of the brain. Visual information from the left side of the

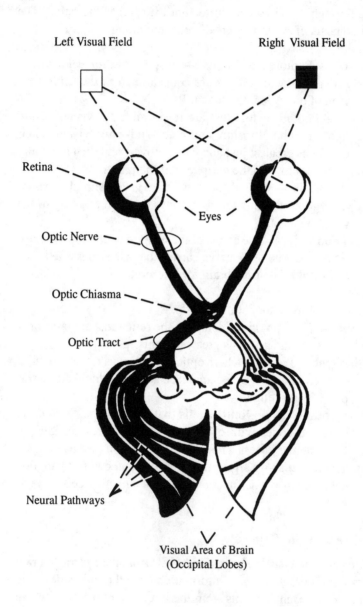

Figure 3.2: Eye to Brain Pathways

visual field exits from the right optic nerves of both eyes, which also meet at the optic chiasma where they are combined and sent to the right side of the brain. In the brain, the visual information is further processed in the **thalamus** and then sent to the visual cortex located in the **occipital lobe** of each hemisphere. The occipital cortex contains cells known as **feature detectors,** including **simple cells** or **edge detectors** which respond to lines or edges, **complex cells** which respond to the motion and color of objects, and **hypercomplex cells** which respond to an object's orientation, movement, shape, corners, width, color, and length.

3.2.4 Light and Dark Adaptation

When entering a darkened room, full **dark adaptation** of the eyes takes place in about 30 to 40 minutes due to a chemical reaction in the rods and cones. The cones adapt first, but they are absolutely **less** sensitive than the rods, so that the absolute threshold for the cones stops decreasing after 10 minutes or so in the dark while the rods continue adapting for 20 or more minutes. The rods cannot discriminate colors, however, and this is why you cannot make out colors in very dim light. When reentering a bright area, the rods quickly lose their dark adaptation and the eyes become **light adapted** as the cones quickly take over.

3.2.5 Color Vision

The three attributes used to describe color are **hue** (determined by wavelength of light; it is the color of visible light), **brightness** (which is a function of the overall intensity of all the wavelengths), and **saturation** (purity or richness of color).

Longer wavelengths of light appear **red** (around 700 nm), **middle wavelengths appear green** (500 nm), and **shorter wavelengths appear blue** (470 nm). **Achromatic colors** cannot be distinguished on the basis of hue. Only **chromatic colors** differ in saturation.

Mixing paints and pigments is **subtractive color mixing** because the two paints being mixed absorb or subtract more wavelengths of light than either one does alone. In subtractive color mixing, yellow mixed with blue results in a green color.

Additive color mixing occurs when beams of light combine. Colored lights **add** their dominant wavelengths to the mixture, stimulating more cones. Both the human eye and color television work according to additive color mixing. Mixing lights produces a color lighter than the darker of the two starting colors. This is why **white** is produced in an additive mixture by mixing all colors together. The **primary colors** of additive mixtures are **red, green, and blue.** These primary colors may be combined in various proportions to match almost all colors. No one primary color can be matched by a mixture of the other two.

For every color, there is another color that is its complement. **Complementary colors** are colors that appear directly opposite one another on the **color circle** and when mixed together in the proper portion, produce a mixture that appears neutral gray. In additive color mixing, yellow and blue are complementary colors and when mixed together, produce gray.

If you stare at a highly saturated patch of color for 20 seconds or so and then look at a white piece of paper, you will see the complementary of the color you were just looking at. When this occurs, it is called a **negative afterimage.**

The **Young-Helmholtz Theory** or **Trichromatic Theory** of color vision proposes that there are three kinds of color receptors in the cones of the eye, one for each of the three primary colors. Physiological data has supported this hypothesis. Three different kinds of cones have been discovered, one sensitive to red light, one sensitive to green light, and one that responds to blue light. According to the Young-Helmholtz Theory, when you look at a **red object,** the red cones are stimulated to send a message to the brain so that you sense redness. All other colors are perceived as a result of the mixture of red, green, or blue cones being stimulated. A **yellow** object, for example, stimulates green and red cones to respond. The color **white** occurs when red, blue, and green cones are stimulated equally, and **black** results from no cone stimulation.

Hering noted that certain kinds of **color blindness** were not well explained by the Young-Helmholtz Theory. The most common form of color blindness is **red-green blindness.** Individuals with red-green blindness find it difficult to sense red or green but have no trouble seeing yellow. This does not agree with the Young-Helmholtz Theory which implies that yellow is a mixture of red and green. Hering argued that yellow was just as much a primary color as red or green or blue and developed the **Opponent-Process Theory** of color vision. The Opponent-Process Theory states that there is a **red-green receptor,** a **yellow-blue receptor,** and a **dark-light** (or black-white) **receptor.** Only one member of a pair can respond, either red *or* green, yellow *or* blue, dark *or* light, but *not* red *and* green or yellow *and* blue. If one member of a receptor pair is stimulated more than its opponent, the corresponding color will be seen. For example, if red is stimulated more than green, the color red will be seen and vice versa. If both members of a pair are stimulated equally, they cancel each other out and this leaves only gray. (Members from nonopponent pairs may interact and be stimulated at the same time, resulting in colors such as yellow-red or blue-green.)

The **Young-Helmholtz Theory** seems to be a good description of visual processing in the **retina** because cones have been found to be sensitive to red, green, and blue (and not to red-green and blue-yellow). The **Opponent-Process Theory** seems to be a better explanation of color vision at higher levels within the brain — at the **optic nerve and beyond.**

3.3 Hearing

The ear functions to convert sound waves from the external environment into nerve impulses which reach the brain and are then transformed into the sensation we know as sound.

3.3.1 Measuring Sound

Sound travels as a series of **invisible waves** in the air. **Frequency** is one **physical dimension** of sound. The frequency of sound is the number of complete waves that pass a given point in space every second and is measured in units called **hertz (Hz).** One cycle per second is 1 Hz. The longer the wavelength, the lower the frequency. The human ear can hear between 20 to 20,000 Hz. A **pure tone** is made up of only one frequency. Frequency determines the **pitch** of a sound (a tone's highness or lowness). Pitch is a **psychological dimension** of sound. It varies with frequency but may also be changed by intensity.

Amplitude is another **physical dimension** of sound and refers to the height of the sound waves. It determines the loudness of sound, which is a **psychological dimension**. The loudness of sound is measured in **decibels (dB)**. The **threshold of hearing** is 0 dB. A whisper is about 25 dB, and a normal conversation is 60 dB. A person could experience hearing loss if exposed to sound over 90 dB for a period of time. Sound over about 130 dB can produce pain. The decibel scale is a **logarithmic** one. Thus, a sound that is 100 dB more intense than another sound is 10 million times more powerful.

3.3.2 Structure of the Ear

A diagram of the human ear is presented in Figure 3.3.

As sound waves travel through the air in the environment, they funnel into the ear where they collide with the **eardrum** or **tympanic membrane** which is like a tight drumhead within the ear canal. Sound waves set the eardrum in motion which causes three small bones, the **auditory ossicles**, to vibrate by means of a chain reaction. First the eardrum causes the **hammer** or **malleus** to vibrate, which in turn sets the **anvil** or **incus** to vibrate, causing the **stirrup** or **stapes** to vibrate. The stirrup is attached to the **oval window**. As the oval window moves back and forth, it sets up waves in the fluid of the **cochlea**, which is a snail-shaped structure that contains the nerve endings essential for hearing. By the time the sound has reached the oval window, it is many times stronger than when it first struck the eardrum. Within the cochlea is the **organ of Corti** which contains about 16,000 hair cells or **cilia**. The movement of the fluid within the cochlea causes the cilia to bend and as they bend, nerve impulses are sent via the auditory nerve to the brain. The neural pathway from the cochlea to the auditory cortex has been described as the most complicated of all sensory pathways.

The ear can be divided into three sections, the **outer ear**, the **middle ear**, and the **inner ear**. In order to hear, the sound wave must enter the outer ear and pass through the middle ear into the inner ear:

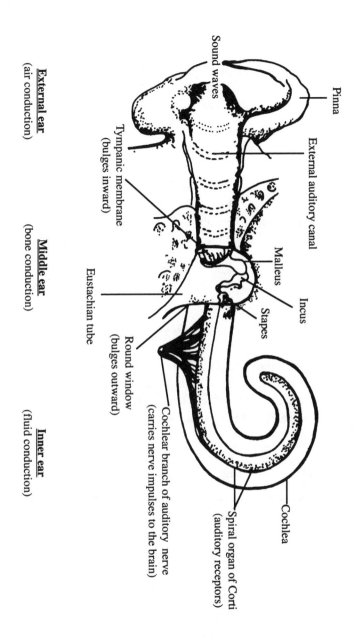

Sound waves

Pinna

Tympanic membrane
(bulges inward)

External auditory canal

Malleus

Incus

Stapes

Eustachian tube

Round window
(bulges outward)

Cochlear branch of auditory nerve
(carries nerve impulses to the brain)

Spiral organ of Corti
(auditory receptors)

Cochlea

External ear
(air conduction)

Middle ear
(bone conduction)

Inner ear
(fluid conduction)

Figure 3.3: Structure of the Auditory System

Outer Ear

Gathers the sound. Sound travels by means of **air conduction.**
Consists of **pinna (external ear)** and **tympanic membrane
(eardrum).**

↓

Middle Ear

Transmits the sound by means of **bone conduction.** Consists of
malleus (hammer), incus (anvil), and **stapes (stirrup).**

↓

Inner Ear

Transforms sound into **neural energy** by means of **fluid
conduction.** Consists of **oval window, cochlea, cilia,
basilar membrane, organ of Corti,** and
semi-circular canals (determine balance).

3.3.3 Theories of Hearing

Several theories have been developed to explain how hearing
works. The main question these theories are attempting to answer is
how neural impulses are coded within the inner ear to give the brain
different kinds of auditory information.

Place theory is based on the idea that different **sound frequencies** actually trigger different neurons. The **basilar membrane** is a
membrane inside the cochlea that is sensitive to frequency differences in sound vibrations. The **middle frequencies** distort the basilar membrane at the **apex** of the cochlea and **high frequencies** distort the basilar membrane at the **base** of the cochlea, near the oval
window. Place theory, therefore, attempts to explain the reception of

sound waves between 5,000 and 20,000 Hz by stating that different frequencies stimulate cilia at different places within the cochlea. Place theory has difficulty explaining tones below 5,000 Hz, however. These **low tones** tend to stimulate cilia throughout the **entire organ of Corti.**

Frequency theory accounts for sounds between 20 and 300 Hz, the **lowest tones** heard by the human ear. Frequency theory asserts that neural activity is coded in terms of the **rate**, rather than the place, at which neurons are triggered. Frequency theory is based on the notion that auditory neurons fire at rates well correlated with the frequency of the sound. Frequency theory cannot, however, account for high-frequency sounds because it is impossible for a single neuron to fire, recover, and fire again as fast as would be necessary to follow a high frequency tone.

Volley theory accounts for tones from 300 to 5,000 Hz (**midrange frequencies**) in which several neurons fire out of sequence in volleys to sum 300 to 5,000 cycles per second. According to this theory, auditory neurons fire in volleys that are correlated with the frequency of the sound.

3.4 The Other Senses

Although vision and hearing are the most studied senses, other senses are important as well.

The four basic **taste** qualities are **sour** (sides of tongue), **sweet** (tip of tongue), **salty** (sides and tip of tongue), and **bitter** (back of tongue).

Taste is a **chemical sense.** The stimuli for taste perception are chemicals absorbed in the saliva that stimulate taste cells located in the **taste buds.** Taste buds are mostly located on the tongue, with a few in the throat. They are replaced about every seven days. Preferences for some tastes appear inborn and others appear learned. Newborn infants respond to sweet, sour, salty, and bitter stimuli, although they prefer sweet. The smell, appearance, temperature, etc. of food also affect how its taste is perceived.

Smell may be one of the oldest senses and is also a **chemical sense.** The receptors for smell are located in the **olfactory epithelium** high up in the roof of the nose. The technical term for smell is

olfaction. Receptors for smell function in a **lock and key** fashion. Different smells have molecules of certain shapes that fit into receptors that are sensitive to them (like keys fit a certain lock), producing a given odor. **Odorless** substances have a molecular shape that does not stimulate receptors in the olfactory epithelium. Smells that excite sexual interest in animals are called **pheromones.** Olfactory messages are *not* relayed through the thalamus, but pass directly to lower areas of the brain that are **older in evolutionary terms.**

Imbedded within the skin are many receptors for **touch.** Different touch receptors measure pressure, light touch, vibration, pain, cold, and warmth. Touch receptors are distributed over the body in **receptive fields,** each associated with its own grouping of touch neurons. Touch receptors are unevenly distributed on the skin. For instance, touch receptors are more highly concentrated on the fingertips than on the back. Touch reception is projected to the **somatosensory area** of the **parietal lobes** of the brain. Different locations in the cerebral cortex receive touch information from different parts on the body.

The **kinesthetic sense** provides us with information about the position of our body in space. The receptors for the sense of kinesthesis are located in the **joints** and **muscles.** Specialized **kinesthetic detectors** in the brain appear to be associated with different postures.

The **vestibular sense** is the sense of **balance.** Its receptors are located in the **semi-circular canals** and **vestibular sacs** located in the **inner ear.** The semi-circular canals are three small, fluid-filled canals located in the inner ear, which contain receptors sensitive to changes in spatial orientation. **Cilia** or **hair cells** in the semi-circular canals are displaced by moving fluid which sends information to the brain about balance and body position. The vestibular sacs are two bag-like structures at the base of the semi-circular canals that also contain receptors for the sense of balance.

CHAPTER 4

Perception

4.1 Depth Perception

Sensation and perception are related because **perception** involves the **interpretation of sensory information.**

Nativists and the **direct perception theory** assert that perception is an **innate** mechanism and is a function of **biological organization.** **Empiricists** and the **image and cue theory** believe that perceptions are **learned** based on past experience.

The **ecological view** of perception argues that perception is an automatic process that is a function of information provided by the environment. The **constructionist view** of perception holds that we construct reality by putting together the bits of information provided by our senses.

Perceptual set is a readiness to perceive a stimulus in a particular way.

Depth perception involves the interpretation of **visual cues** in order to determine **how far away** objects are.

There is currently a debate as to whether depth perception is an **inborn ability** or a **learned response** as a result of experience (**nature vs. nurture**).

Gibson and **Walk** (1960) developed an apparatus they called the **visual cliff** that is used to measure depth perception in infants and toddlers. The visual cliff consists of an elevated glass platform divided into two sections. One section has a surface that is textured with a checkerboard pattern of tile, while the other has a clear glass surface with a checkerboard pattern several feet below it so it looks like the floor drops off. Gibson and Walk hypothesized that if infants can perceive depth, they should remain on the "shallow" side of the platform and avoid the "cliff" side, even if coaxed to come across by parents. When they tested infants from 6 to 14 months of age, Gibson and Walk found that infants would crawl or walk to their mothers when the mothers were on the "shallow" side of the platform, but would refuse to cross the "deep" side even with their mothers' encouragements to cross. The results of this and other visual cliff studies still do not prove that depth perception is innate because before infants can be tested, they must be able to crawl and may have already learned to avoid drop-offs.

Two types of visual cues, binocular cues and monocular cues, allow us to perceive depth.

4.1.1 Binocular Cues

Binocular cues for depth require the use of **both eyes.** The two binocular cues are convergence and retinal disparity.

Convergence involves the interpretation of **muscular movements** related to how close or how far away an object is. For an object closer than approximately 25 feet, our eyes must converge (move inward) in order to perceive it as a single object clearly in focus. Our perceptual system uses this muscular movement as a cue for closeness. For an object farther than 25 feet, our eyes tend to focus on infinity (little to no muscular movement required), and again, our perceptual system uses this as a cue that the object must be far away.

Retinal disparity is the difference in locations, on the retinas, of the stimulation by a single object. This means that an object viewed by both eyes will stimulate one spot on the right retina and a different spot on the left retina. This is due to the fact that the object is at a different distance from each eye. Retinal disparity is also used as a cue for depth because the **eyes are set a certain distance apart** in the head, and objects closer than 25 feet are sensed on significantly different locations **on each eye's retina.** Viewing objects that are close causes considerable retinal disparity (very different portions of each retina are stimulated) and viewing objects at a distance creates **little** retinal disparity (similar portions of each retina are stimulated).

4.1.2 Monocular Cues

Monocular cues for depth require the use of **only one eye.** Two-dimensional presentations (e.g., photographs, television) also rely on monocular cues to indicate depth.

Monocular cues for depth include:

Linear Perspective — Parallel lines appear to converge on the horizon (e.g., railroad tracks).

Relative Size — Closer objects appear larger; the larger of two figures will always appear closer because the two objects will project retinal images of different sizes.

Overlap or Interposition — Objects that are overlapped or partially concealed by other objects will appear farther away.

Gradient of Texture — Objects that are closer have greater detail or texture than those far away.

Aerial Perspective — Close objects are bright and sharp; distant objects are pastel and hazy.

Relative Motion or Motion Parallax — When moving our head from side to side, nearby objects appear to move more than distant objects; far objects appear to move slower than nearby objects.

Height on a Plane or Height in a Field — Objects that are closer appear to be lower in the field than objects that are farther away.

Looming Effect or Optical Expansion — When we approach objects, objects close to us appear to be moving toward us faster than those farther away.

Accommodation — Lens of eye must bend or adjust to bring to focus objects that are relatively close (see Chapter 3).

4.2 Perceptual Organization

We tend to **organize** our sensations into meaningful perceptions. Perceptual organization is the basis of **Gestalt Psychology.** Gestalt psychologists assert that we tend to organize our perceptions immediately into **wholes,** and emphasize that the whole is **greater than** the sum of its parts.

Gestaltists have presented a number of descriptive principles of perceptual organization:

Figure-ground — We group some sensations into an object or "figure" that stands out on a plain background. The figure is the distinct shape with clearly defined edges and the ground has no defined edges. **Reversible** or **ambiguous figures** have no clearly defined figures and backgrounds (the figure and background can be reversed).

Similarity — Stimuli that are similar in size, shape, color, or form tend to be grouped together.

Nearness or Proximity — Stimuli that are near each other tend to be grouped together.

Continuity — Perceptions tend toward simplicity or continuity; lines tend to be seen as following the smoothest path; lines interrupted by an overlapping object are seen as belonging together if they result in straight or gently curving lines when connected.

Closure — Figures that have gaps in them are seen as completed and are perceived as recognizable figures.

Common Fate — Objects that move together tend to be grouped together.

Simplicity — Every stimulus pattern is perceived in such a way that the resulting structure is as simple as possible.

Orientation — Objects with the same orientation are seen as part of a group.

Apparent Motion or Phi Phenomenon — Perceived motion when the object is, in fact, stationary. (For example, when two lights are placed side by side in a darkened room and flashed alternately, one light moving back and forth is perceived.)

4.3 Perceptual Constancies

Another important characteristic of visual perception is the **per-**

ceptual constancy or stability of the shape, size, brightness, and color of objects in our visual fields. We are able to recognize the same objects at a variety of angles, at various distances, and even under different colored lighting because of perceptual constancies:

Size Constancy — Objects we are familiar with seem to appear the same size despite changes in the distance between us and the objects.

Shape Constancy — Objects appear to be the same shape despite changes in their orientation toward the viewer.

Brightness or Lightness Constancy — Objects appear to stay the same brightness despite changes in the amount of light falling on them.

Color Constancy — The hue of an object appears to stay the same despite changes in background lighting.

4.4 Perceptual Illusions

An **illusion** is an **incorrect** or **inaccurate perception** of the stimulus being presented. An illusion is *not* the same as an **hallucination** where there is *no* stimulus being perceived.

There is evidence that **learning** might have an important bearing on the perception of illusions. There are individual differences in how (and how strongly) illusions are perceived, and illusions tend to diminish in effect the more you observe them.

Psychologists study illusions because they help us understand underlying perceptual processes. Illusions occur because of cues in the environment. Motivation, expectancy, and/or experiences "trick" us into perceiving things incorrectly.

Some common visual illusions are presented in Figure 4.1. These and other illusions are described below.

In the **Ponzo illusion,** the top horizontal line appears to be longer when, in fact, it is identical in length to the bottom line. Because the top line appears farther away, the principle of **size constancy** as well as the **size distance hypothesis** help explain this illusion. The size distance hypothesis is based on size constancy and states that if two objects project the same retinal image but appear at different distances from the viewer, the object that appears farther away from the

37

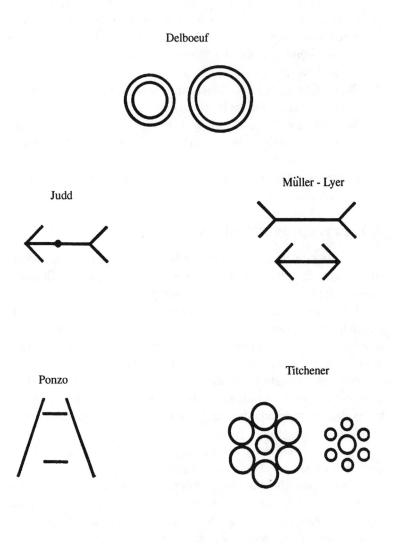

Figure 4.1: Visual Illusions

viewer will typically be perceived as larger. Because the top line in the Ponzo illusion looks farther away (because of linear perspective) than the bottom line, we perceive the distant line to be longer.

The center horizontal lines in both figures of the **Müller-Lyer illusion** are the same length, but the one in the top figure is perceived as longer. This is because the apparent length of both straight lines is distorted by the arrowheads added to the ends. The same is true for the **Judd illusion** where the line segments on either side of the center dot are actually equal in length.

The **Titchener illusion** occurs because of **comparative size**. The center circle of the figure on the left looks smaller than the corresponding center circle of the figure on the right even though they are both the same size. The center circles are perceived incorrectly because of the comparisons made relative to their surrounding circles. The same is true for the **Delboeuf illusion** where the outer circle of the left figure is actually identical to the inner circle of the figure on the right.

The **moon illusion** refers to the phenomenon of the moon appearing larger when it is viewed at the horizon than at the zenith, even though both retinal images are identical. The moon illusion can be explained by the **size distance hypothesis**. Because the apparent shape of the sky is flattened when viewing a moon at the horizon, this may make the moon appear farther away and thus larger.

CHAPTER 5

States of Consciousness

5.1 Sleeping and Consciousness

Consciousness includes not only our awareness of stimuli in the external environment but also our recognition of internal events, such as what we are thinking, an increased heart rate, pain, etc. Consciousness is, therefore, our continually changing stream of mental activity.

The **active mode** of consciousness involves **controlled** or **heightened awareness** and involves planning, making decisions, and responding to those decisions. The **passive mode** of consciousness relates to **minimal awareness** and includes daydreaming and sleeping.

Altered states of consciousness occur any time the content or quality of conscious experience undergoes a significant change. Most research on altered states of consciousness has focused on sleep, dreams, hypnosis, meditation, and the use of psychoactive substances or drugs.

Sleep is defined as a state of unresponsiveness from which we can be aroused relatively easily.

5.1.1 Circadian Rhythms

Circadian rhythm or biological clock refers to a person's daily sleep and wakefulness cycle that appears to be controlled, at least in part, in an area of the **hypothalamus** called the **suprachiasmatic nucleus.**

External cues can also influence circadian rhythms. Such cues include the light and dark of day and night.

The high point of wakefulness is related to **increased** body temperature and cortisol levels, with vision, hearing, smell, taste, and alertness at their peak.

The low point of wakefulness is related to **decreased** body temperature and cortisol levels and increased sleepiness.

The tendency to adopt a **25-hour cycle** (instead of 24-hour) and as a result go to sleep later and later on succeeding nights is known as **free-running.** This tends to happen when there are no time cues available.

Jet lag occurs when there is a discrepancy between our biological clock and the official clock. Traveling across time zones creates this discrepancy and can result in fitful sleep and a sluggish feeling.

5.1.2 Sleep Patterns

All animals seem to need sleep but in varying amounts. For example, a cat sleeps, on average, 14 hours per day. An elephant sleeps only 2 to 4 hours per day. The average adult human sleeps around 7 to 8 hours. Human infants spend around 16 hours per day sleeping, though this amount decreases as they get older. After the age of 70, the average person sleeps about 6 hours per day. **Healthy insomniacs** can get by on as little as 3 hours of sleep per day.

Researchers have not found many systematic differences between those who habitually sleep more or less each day.

5.1.3 Stages of Sleep

The same stages of sleep appear in all mammals, although the pattern may vary.

Our brain waves, as measured by **EEG patterns,** vary depending on our state of consciousness. For instance, **EEG beta waves** are associated with being awake. Generally, as we move from an awake state through deeper stages of sleep, our brain waves **decrease in frequency** (cycles per second) and **increase in amplitude** (height).

41

Researchers have found that when we sleep, we cycle through a series of five distinct states:

Alpha Waves — Drowsy but awake state when the eyes are closed and relaxed.

Stage 1 Sleep — Transition between wakefulness and real sleep. **Theta waves.** EEG pattern changes to small, irregular pattern. After 5-10 minutes, move on to Stage 2. Wake up in this stage of sleep.

Stage 2 Sleep — Sleep **spindles** occur. Muscles less tense, eyes rest. Larger EEG **theta waves.** After 10 minutes, go on to Stage 3. Half of our sleep time is in Stage 2.

Stage 3 Sleep — EEG **delta waves** appear about 50 percent of time. Slow-wave sleep.

Stage 4 Sleep — Over half the waves are **delta.** Most difficult to awaken from; deepest sleep. Decreases with age.

We spend the first 30 to 45 minutes going from Stage 1 to Stage 4 sleep. The next 30 to 45 minutes is spent reversing the direction, from Stage 4 back to Stage 1. At this point, **REM sleep** occurs.

REM or **rapid eye movement** sleep is sometimes referred to as **paradoxical sleep** or **active sleep** because although individuals are asleep, their EEG patterns resemble those of someone who is active and awake. Heart rate, respiration, blood pressure, and other physiological patterns are like those occurring during the day. There is also a loss of muscle tone or paralysis called **atonia** during REM sleep. Most of our **dreaming** also occurs during REM sleep. Atonia during REM sleep may keep sleepers from acting out their dreams.

Sleepers are hard to awaken from REM sleep and will often incorporate an unexpected sound from their environment (e.g., alarm clock) into their dreams. This may be one way of avoiding REM sleep disruption.

When deprived of REM sleep, **REM rebound** can occur whereby the sleeper will drop into REM sleep very soon after falling asleep on subsequent nights and will engage in more REM sleep than usual.

Non-REM sleep (NREM) does not include rapid eye movements and is sometimes referred to as **orthodox sleep.** NREM sleep consists of sleeping hours when REM sleep is not occurring. Few dreams occur during NREM sleep. Sleeptalking and sleepwalking occur during NREM sleep.

During the night, we travel back and forth through the stages of sleep four to six times. Each completed cycle takes about 90 minutes. During the first half of the night, most of the time is spent in deeper sleep and only a few minutes in REM. The last half of the night is dominated by Stage 2 and REM sleep, from which we wake up.

Both the total amount of sleep per night and the proportion of REM sleep change with age. We tend to sleep less as we get older and the total amount of REM sleep decreases. Infants spend about eight hours per day in REM sleep; adults spend about one to two hours per day in REM sleep.

5.1.4 Theories of Sleep

Several theories attempt to answer the question of why we need to sleep.

The **adaptive theory** states that each species needs a certain amount of time awake in order to survive and that sleep is an adaptive mechanism that protects members of a species by keeping them out of trouble during time not devoted to survival activities (e.g., eating).

The **conserving energy theory** argues that sleep is a protective method for conserving energy because we burn fewer calories while sleeping.

The **restorative function theory** states that sleep is necessary for resting and restoring the body, for nervous system development, and for consolidating what has been learned during the day.

5.1.5 Sleep Disorders

Many people are troubled by sleep disorders. Sleep disorders include:

Insomnia — Either have difficulty *falling* asleep or problems *staying* asleep. Causes include depression, drugs or alcohol, irregular circadian rhythm (e.g., jet lag), or stress. Treatments include medication and going to bed and arising at the same time each day.

Narcolepsy — Uncontrollable, recurring, sudden onset of REM sleep. Total loss of muscle control. Most likely to occur during moments of anxiety or stress. Exact cause unknown. Associated with disturbances in brain stem. Medication is usual treatment.

Sleep Apnea — Frequent stoppages of breathing during sleep that last at least 20 seconds. Sleep is interrupted to restore breathing. Can result in heavy snoring, snorting, and daytime sleepiness. Rarely realize breathing has stopped.

Night Terror — Sudden awakening in which sleeper may sit up, eyes open with a look of terror, and may scream. Occurs during NREM sleep. Usually not remembered in morning.

Hypersomnia — Excessive sleep; more than 12 hours per day. Great difficulty awakening and feel drowsy throughout day. Causes include severe depression, drug dependence, and physical disorders.

Sleepwalking or Somnambulism — Walking or sitting up in bed during NREM sleep. Eyes may be open but are unseeing. Sleepwalker lacks critical judgment.

Sleeptalking — Talking during NREM sleep. Speech usually not understandable. More common in children.

Nightmares — Disturbing dreams that occur during REM sleep.

5.2 Dreaming

Dreaming is a mental experience that occurs during sleep and consists of vivid images. While we dream, we accept bizarre happenings without question. Most dreaming occurs during REM sleep. **Lucid dreaming** occurs when a sleeper is aware of dreaming while a dream is happening.

There are different theories concerning what dreams are:

Psychoanalytic Theory — Dreams are repressed desires and provide access to the unconscious in symbolic form. Sexual and aggressive impulses are disguised in our dreams.

Activation-Synthesis Model — Dreaming is the brain's attempt to make sense out of random electrical activity that enters the forebrain during REM sleep. Dreams are a response to this random electrical activity and have no meaning.

Housekeeping Hypothesis — The cleaning up or clearing out of unneeded neural connections occurs during dreaming, which is why the brain creates the random electrical activity.

Off-Line Hypothesis — REM sleep plays a role in learning by integrating new and old information.

5.3 Hypnosis

Hypnosis comes from the Greek word **hypnos,** meaning "sleep." Hypnotized people, however, are not asleep.

Franz Anton Mesmer (1734-1815), an Austrian physician, popularized **mesmerism** (now called hypnosis) in order to cure patients.

Hypnosis is a systematic procedure used to produce a heightened state of suggestibility. Hypnosis can lead to enhanced fantasy and role-taking abilities, reduced reality testing and planfulness, and redistributed attention.

Posthypnotic suggestions are suggestions made during hypnosis that influence a person's later behavior. **Posthypnotic amnesia** occurs when hypnotized subjects are told they will remember nothing that happened while they were hypnotized.

Age regression is a term that describes hypnotized subjects who are behaving as if they are reliving experiences from childhood.

Dissociation involves the splitting off of mental processes into two separate, simultaneous streams of awareness. Hypnotized subjects can then perform acts that do not register in their conscious memory or can engage in two behaviors while remembering only one of them. **Automatic writing** is an example of dissociation and occurs when a hypnotized subject writes something without being aware of it and while discussing something else.

Dissociation Theory states that hypnosis is a splitting of central control of thought processes and behavior. The hypnotized subject agrees to give some control to the hypnotist.

According to **role theory,** people play the role of being hypnotized and thus comply with the hypnotist's directions.

State theory says that hypnosis is a special state of consciousness and that significant changes in basic mental processes take place during hypnosis.

Self-hypnosis occurs without the aid of a hypnotist. **Highway hypnosis** is a form of self-hypnosis that can occur while driving a car. People can drive great distances with no conscious memory of responding to traffic signals, other cars, etc.

Not everyone can be hypnotized. Special tests, such as the **Hypnotic Susceptibility Scale**, can measure how **susceptible** one is to hypnosis. Individuals most susceptible to hypnosis tend to have active imaginations, good concentrative ability, proneness to fantasy, and a favorable opinion of hypnosis. **Willingness** to be hypnotized is also an important factor.

Hypnosis is used as a substitute for **anesthetic drugs** and to help control pain by some patients.

Hypnosis cannot directly improve memory; it can be used, however, to reduce anxiety that may inhibit remembering.

5.4 Meditation

Meditation includes a group of techniques that attempt to focus attention and promote relaxation. It involves a deliberate attempt to alter consciousness.

Concentrative meditation involves focusing all attention on one thing — one word, one item, one sound, etc. — while sitting back and breathing deeply. This results in the same information being cycled through the nervous system repeatedly. The goal is to become nonresponsive to the external environment.

Early researchers reported that meditation produces decreased heart rate, blood pressure, and oxygen consumption as well as increased body temperature at the extremities and muscle relaxation. EEG **alpha waves** become more prominent. Later researchers concluded that meditation is no more effective than other relaxation techniques.

5.5 Drugs

Drugs are also used in deliberate attempts to alter one's state of consciousness. The drugs that people use **recreationally** are psychoactive. **Psychoactive drugs** are chemical substances that influence the brain, alter consciousness, and produce psychological changes.

Drug abuse or **recreational drug use** is the self-administration of drugs in ways that deviate from either the medical or social norms of a society. **Addiction** is a **physical dependence** in which continued use of a psychoactive drug is necessary to prevent withdrawal symptoms. **Withdrawal symptoms** vary with different drugs, but may include nausea, headache, chills, and craving for the drug. **Avoiding** these withdrawal symptoms **motivates** an addicted person to continue using the drug. **Tolerance** refers to a person's progressively decreasing responsiveness to a drug, leading to increased amounts of the drug being required to produce the same effect. Most drugs produce tolerance effects, but they vary in how rapidly they occur.

Psychological dependence can occur without addiction and exists when one must continue to take a drug in order to satisfy mental and emotional cravings for the drug. The psychological pleasure received from using the drug is what **motivates** a person who is psychologically dependent.

Several **major categories** of psychoactive drugs, including depressants, stimulants, hallucinogens, and narcotics, are discussed in the next sections.

5.5.1 Depressants

Depressants or **sedatives** are drugs that depress the functioning of the central nervous system.

Examples:
Alcohol, Barbiturates (e.g., Seconal, Nembutal), and **Tranquilizers** (e.g., Valium, Librium, Xanax).

Methods of administration:
Oral or injected.

Main effects:
Alcohol at first produces mild euphoria, relaxation, and lowered inhibitions. As the dose increases, more of the brain's activity is impaired,

47

resulting eventually in sleep, or with increased consumption, even death.

Barbiturates or **"downers"** have a calming, sedative effect; they can reduce inhibitions and promote sleep.

Tranquilizers lower anxiety and also have a calming, sedative effect. They promote relaxation and work with the neurotransmitter **GABA,** which is associated with inhibitory synapses.

Medical uses:
　　Alcohol can be used as an antiseptic.
　　Barbiturates are used as sleeping pills or as anticonvulsants.
　　Tranquilizers are prescribed to lower anxiety.

Side effects:
　　Impaired coordination, increased urination, emotional swings, depression, impaired judgment, quarrelsomeness, and hangover are some potential side effects of the consumption of **alcohol.**
　　For **barbiturates,** side effects include impaired coordination and reflexes, and drowsiness.
　　Side effects of **tranquilizers** are lethargy, sleepiness, and decreased muscular tension.

Potential for addiction/psychological dependence:
　　Alcohol: High/High.
　　Barbiturates: High/High.
　　Tranquilizers: Moderate to High/High.

Withdrawal symptoms:
　　For **alcohol,** withdrawal symptoms include tremors, nausea, sweating, depression, irritability, and hallucinations.
　　Withdrawal symptoms for **barbiturates** are trouble sleeping, anxiety, seizures, cardiovascular collapse, and even death.
　　For **tranquilizers,** restlessness, anxiety, irritability, muscle tension, and trouble sleeping are possible withdrawal symptoms.

5.5.2 Stimulants

　　Stimulants increase central nervous system activity.

Examples:
Nicotine, Caffeine, Amphetamines (e.g., Benzedrine, Dexedrine, Methadrine), and **Cocaine.**

Methods of administration:
Oral, sniffed, injected, smoked, and freebased.

Main effects:
Nicotine increases metabolic processes (e.g., pulse rate), lowers carbohydrate appetite, and can produce alertness or calmness.
Caffeine promotes wakefulness and increases metabolism but slows reaction times.
Amphetamines (e.g., "speed," "uppers") stimulate neurotransmission at the synapse. Both the central nervous system and the sympathetic branch in the autonomic nervous system are affected. They can increase energy and excitement and reduce fatigue and appetite.
Cocaine increases feelings of excitement and a euphoric mood, boosts energy, and acts as an appetite suppressant.

Medical uses:
Stimulants are used in the treatment of hyperactivity and narcolepsy. **Cocaine** has been used as a local anesthetic.

Side effects:
The main side effects of stimulants include increased pulse and blood pressure, restlessness, reduced appetite, increased sweating and urination, insomnia, and increased aggressiveness.

Potential for addiction/psychological dependence:
Nicotine: High/Moderate to high.
Caffeine: Moderate/Moderate.
Amphetamines: Moderate/High.
Cocaine: Moderate to high/High.

Withdrawal symptoms:
Nicotine: Anxiety, increased appetite, and irritability.
Caffeine: Headache and depression.

Amphetamines: Increased appetite, depression, sleeping for long periods, fatigue, and irritability.

Cocaine: Sleeping for long periods, fatigue, irritability, increased appetite, and depression.

5.5.3 Hallucinogens

Hallucinogens ("psychedelic drugs") are chemical substances that alter perceptions of reality and may cause hallucinations and other distortions in sensory and perceptual experiences.

Examples:
Several synthetic drugs, such as **LSD (lysergic acid diethylamide)** and **PCP (phencyclidine)**, as well as substances extracted from plants, such as **Marijuana.**

Methods of administration:
Smoked, snorted, or swallowed.

Main effects:
LSD is derived from a fungus **(ergot)** that grows on rye. Even small doses (i.e., 10 micrograms) can produce effects that last for hours and include, mild euphoria, hallucinations, body image alterations, loss of control of one's attention, and insightful experiences or "mind expansion."

PCP is an **anesthetic** often called **"angel dust."** It works by binding to the potassium channels in the brain and muscle-activating neurons. May cause loss of contact with reality, aggressive behavior, hallucinations, and insensitivity to pain.

Marijuana is a mixture of leaves, flowers, and stems from the **hemp** plant. Its active ingredient is **tetrahydrocannabinol** or **THC.** When smoked, THC enters the bloodstream through the lungs and reaches peak concentrations in 10 to 30 minutes and its effects may last for several hours. It generally produces euphoria and relaxation, and in sufficient doses, can produce hallucinations. In addition to being a hallucinogen, marijuana is also a **stimulant at higher doses** and a **depressant at lower doses.**

Medical uses:
Most hallucinogens have no medical uses; marijuana, however, has been used in the treatment of glaucoma. Its use in the treatment of HIV and nausea from chemotherapy is under study.

Side effects:
LSD: Possible panic reactions, anxiety, dilated pupils, paranoia, and jumbled thought processes.
PCP: Violent and bizarre behaviors.
Marijuana: Dry mouth, bloodshot eyes, poor motor coordination, memory problems, and anxiety.

Potential for addiction/psychological dependence:
LSD: Low/Low.
PCP: Unknown/High.
Marijuana: Low/Moderate.

Withdrawal symptoms:
Possible withdrawal symptoms for the hallucinogens include anxiety, difficulty sleeping, hyperactivity, and decreased appetite.

5.5.4 Narcotics

Narcotics, also referred to as **opiates** or **analgesics**, are used to relieve pain and induce sleep.

Examples:
Opium, Morphine (e.g., Percodan, Demoral), and **Heroin**.

Methods of administration:
Oral, injected, or smoked.

Main effects:
Opium is an unrefined extract of the poppy seed pod.
Morphine is a refined extract of opium and is stronger in its effects.
Heroin is derived from morphine and is even more potent in its pure form.

Because these narcotic drugs are all derived from opium, they reduce pain by blocking neurotransmission. Narcotics appear to reduce pain because they are chemically similar to the body's own natural opiates. They fit into the body's own opiate receptors and mimic their effects thereby stopping pain from reaching the cortex. Immediately after injection, opiates produce a pronounced feeling of intoxication and euphoria and physical pain is relieved.

Medical uses:
Relief of pain.

Side effects:
The opiates seem to block so many afferent impulses in the brain that not only is pain blocked but also hunger, anxiety, and motivation. Constipation, nausea, and impaired coordination are other possible side effects.

Potential for addiction/psychological dependence:
Opium: High/High.
Morphine: High/High.
Heroin: High/High.

Withdrawal symptoms:
Symptoms of withdrawal from narcotic addiction include diarrhea, chills, sweating, runny nose, muscle spasms, restlessness, and anxiety.

CHAPTER 6

Conditioning and Learning

6.1 Classical Conditioning

Learning is defined as a relative permanent change in behavior as a result of experience, practice, or both. **Conditioning** is the process of forming associations. Learning and conditioning are inferred from behavior because they cannot be observed directly.

Classical conditioning always involves a **reflexive** or **respondent behavior.** This means that classical conditioning produces an automatic response to a stimulus. **Classical** or **respondent conditioning** occurs when a neutral stimulus that does not trigger a reflexive behavior is **conditioned** so that it will elicit an automatic response. Conditioning occurs because the neutral stimulus has been **associated** with a stimulus that automatically triggers a response.

It appears that both humans and animals may be **biologically prepared** to learn some associations more readily than others. The associations that are more readily learned may be ones that increase chances for survival.

Ivan Pavlov (1849-1936), a Russian physiologist, classically conditioned dogs using the **salivary reflex.** Dogs normally respond to food by salivating. They do *not* have to be conditioned to salivate to food. Dogs do not, however, automatically salivate to the sound of a bell ringing. This is what Pavlov conditioned them to do. He would ring the bell, present the food, and the dogs would salivate. He repeated this procedure until the bell alone would cause the dogs to salivate. They had learned to **associate** the sound of the bell with the presentation of food.

The terms used to describe classical conditioning include:

Unconditioned Stimulus (UCS) — The stimulus that automatically produces a reflex. (In Pavlov's study this was the food.)

Unconditioned Response (UCR) — An automatic response to the UCS; a natural response that does not require conditioning for it to occur. (In Pavlov's study this was salivation to the food.)

Conditioned Stimulus (CS) — A neutral stimulus that does not normally elicit an automatic response; only after pairing it repeatedly with the UCS, does the CS come to elicit a conditioned response. (In Pavlov's study this was the bell.)

Conditioned Response (CR) — The learned response that occurs when the CS is presented alone, without the UCS. (In Pavlov's study, the CR was salivation that occurred to the bell alone; no food was present.)

The standard classical conditioning paradigm is:

		UCS (food)	→	**UCR** (salivation)
CS (bell)	**+**	**UCS** (food)	→	**UCR** (salivation)
		CS alone (bell alone)	→	**CR** (salivation)

Step 2 is repeated until the CS alone will prompt the CR.

The timing or **temporal relationship** between the conditioned stimulus (CS) and unconditioned stimulus (UCS) can vary:

Forward pairing — CS presented before UCS

Backward pairing — CS presented after UCS

Simultaneous pairing — CS and UCS occur at exactly the same time.

Research has indicated that forward conditioning leads to the best conditioning, especially if the CS precedes the UCS by about half a second. Backward and simultaneous conditioning are much less effective.

After classical conditioning has taken place, the conditioned stimulus (CS) must be paired with or **reinforced** by the unconditioned stimulus (UCS) at least some of the time or else the conditioned response (CR) will disappear. The process of eliminating the conditioned response (CR) by no longer pairing the unconditioned stimulus (UCS) with the conditioned stimulus (CS) is called **extinction.** Extinction will take place, therefore, if the conditioned stimulus (CS) is presented repeatedly without the unconditioned stimulus (UCS). Extinction is a method that is used intentionally to eliminate conditioned responses (CR).

The conditioned response might recover, however, if a rest period or break follows extinction. A **rest period** would occur if the conditioned stimulus (CS) is *not* presented for a period of time. After this rest period, the very next time the conditioned stimulus (CS) is presented, the conditioned response (CR) is likely to occur (even though it was previously extinguished). If the conditioned response (CR) does reappear, this is called **spontaneous recovery.** Spontaneous recovery is, therefore, the reoccurrence of a conditioned response (CR) after a rest interval has followed extinction.

Figure 6.1 shows the acquisition, extinction, and spontaneous recovery of a conditioned response (CR).

Reconditioning occurs after extinction has taken place and the conditioned stimulus (CS) and unconditioned stimulus (UCS) are again paired. Learning (i.e., responding with a CR when the CS is presented) is usually quicker during reconditioning than it was during initial conditioning.

Stimulus generalization occurs when a conditioned response (CR) occurs to a stimulus that only **resembles** or is **similar** to the conditioned stimulus (CS) but is *not* identical to it. For instance,

55

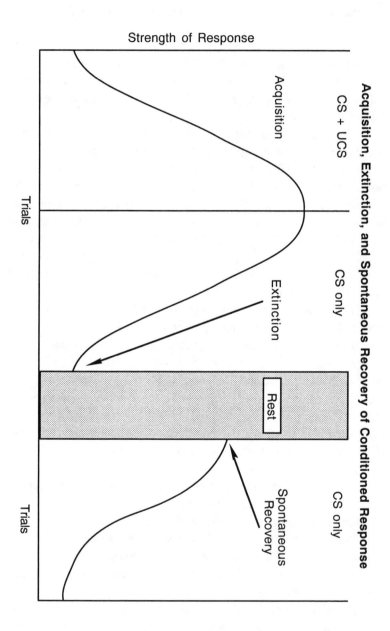

Figure 6.1

Pavlov's dogs were classically conditioned to salivate to a bell (the CS), but if the first time they heard a buzzer they also salivated, this would be stimulus generalization. They were never conditioned with the buzzer, but they responded because the sound resembled that of the bell.

Stimulus discrimination occurs when the differences between stimuli are noticed and, thus, the stimuli are *not* responded to in similar ways. For instance, stimulus discrimination would occur if Pavlov's dogs did *not* salivate to the sound of the buzzer, even if it sounded similar to the bell. This would indicate that the dogs could discriminate these two sounds and as a result, responded differently to each.

Researchers have used humans as well as animals in classical conditioning studies. In humans, emotional reactions occur sometimes as a result of classical conditioning because emotions are involuntary, automatic responses. For instance, **phobias** (intense, irrational fears) may develop as a result of classical conditioning.

The most famous classical conditioning study using a human subject was one conducted by American researcher **John Watson** (1878-1958). Although this study is considered unethical today and some have suggested that it is more myth or legend than fact, most textbooks mention the Little Albert study when discussing classical conditioning. Little Albert was an 11-month old infant who initially was not afraid of laboratory white rats. Watson classically conditioned Albert to fear these rats by pairing the presentation of the rat with a loud noise that scared the infant. The diagram of this study would be:

Noise	→	**Fear response**
(UCS)		(UCR)

Rat +	**Noise**	→	**Fear response**
(CS)	(UCS)		(UCR)

eventually,

Rat alone	→	**Fear response**
(CS)		(CR)

Higher order conditioning occurs when a new neutral stimulus is associated with a conditioned stimulus (CS) and eventually comes to produce the conditioned response (CR). If after Albert was classically conditioned, a dog was always paired with the rat, eventually Albert would display the fear response to the dog. A diagram of this higher order conditioning example would be:

	Rat alone	→	**Fear**
	(CS)		(CR)

Dog +	**Rat alone**	→	**Fear**
(new	(CS)		(CR)
stimulus)			

eventually,

	Dog alone	→	**Fear**
	(CS)		(CR)

6.2   Operant and Instrumental Conditioning

In **operant** or **instrumental conditioning,** responses are learned because of their consequences. Unlike classical conditioning, the responses learned in operant/instrumental conditioning are **voluntary.**

There are subtle measurement differences between operant and instrumental conditioning. Because both of these are similar in most respects, however, the term operant conditioning will be used to refer to both.

American psychologist **Edward L. Thorndike's** (1874-1949) **Law of Effect** states that a behavior that is rewarded tends to be repeated, while behavior that is not rewarded takes place only at random. What is learned during operant or instrumental conditioning is that certain responses are instrumental in producing desired effects in the environment.

Reinforcers are consequences for behavior and can be anything that increases the likelihood that a behavior will be repeated. Reinforcers can be positive or negative. Both positive and negative reinforcers have the potential to **increase behaviors. Positive reinforcers** are rewards or other positive consequences that follow behaviors and increase the likelihood that the behaviors will occur again in the future. Giving your dog a biscuit each time he sits on command is an example of positive reinforcement.

Negative reinforcers are anything a subject will work to avoid or terminate. Nagging behaviors are examples of negative reinforcement because we often will do something (anything!) to stop the nagging. For instance, a parent who buys a child a candy bar to stop a child's nagging in the grocery store is responding to negative reinforcement. **Escape conditioning** occurs when a subject learns that a particular response will terminate an aversive stimulus. The parent who buys a nagging child candy has escaped the nagging by purchasing candy. **Avoidance conditioning** occurs when a subject responds to a signal in a way that prevents exposure to an aversive stimulus. The candy counter at the store may become a signal that parents should buy candy if they want to avoid or prevent their child's nagging.

Reinforcers can also be primary or secondary. **Primary reinforcers** are necessary to meet biological needs and include such things as food, water, air, etc. **Secondary reinforcers** have acquired value and are not necessary for survival. Grades, money, pat on the back, etc. are examples of secondary reinforcers.

A reinforcer becomes less effective in promoting future behavior the longer the delay between a behavior and its reinforcement. The declining effectiveness of reinforcement with increasing delay is called the **gradient of reinforcement.**

Extinction can also occur in operant conditioning. The goal is the same as it is in classical conditioning, to decrease or eliminate a response. Extinction occurs in operant conditioning by removing the reinforcer. For example, the dog stops receiving dog biscuits for sitting or the child gets no candy for nagging. Once these reinforcers are removed, both sitting and nagging should decrease and/or be eliminated. **Spontaneous recovery** can also occur in operant conditioning.

How easily an operant response is extinguished is dependent, in part, on how often that response was reinforced or its **schedule of reinforcement**. A **continuous schedule** of reinforcement happens when each and every response is reinforced (100 percent of the time). *Each* time your dog sits on command, he receives a biscuit. Behaviors that are continuously reinforced are easier to extinguish than behaviors that are not reinforced 100 percent of the time.

Behaviors that are *not* reinforced each time they occur are on an **intermittent** or **partial schedule of reinforcement**. There are four possible partial schedules of reinforcement:

Fixed ratio schedule: Reinforcement is given after a fixed number of responses (e.g., every third time your dog sits, he receives a biscuit). Being paid on a piece-rate basis is an example of a fixed ratio schedule. The fixed ratio schedule produces a high rate of responding with a slight pause after each reinforcement is given. Fixed ratio schedules produce the fastest rate of extinction because the subject realizes quickly that reinforcement has stopped.

Variable ratio schedule: Reinforcement is given after a variable number of responses. Thus, on one occasion, reinforcement may occur after 10 responses and on another occasion after 50, etc. The rate of reinforcement depends upon the rate of responding: the faster, the more reinforcers received. This schedule produces steady, high rates of responding and is extremely resistant to extinction. Slot machines are based on variable ratio schedules.

Fixed interval schedule: Reinforcement is given after the first response after a given amount of time has elapsed. This may mean a reinforcer every five minutes, for example. Being paid once per month is another example. Fixed interval schedules produce a low rate of responding at the beginning of each interval and a high rate toward the end of each interval.

Variable interval schedule: Reinforcement is given after the first response after a varying amount of time has elapsed. Pop quizzes often occur on a variable interval schedule. The variable interval schedule produces a steady, slow rate of responding.

In general, the ratio schedules produce higher response rates than the interval schedules. Variable schedules are usually harder to extinguish than are fixed schedules because variable schedules are less predictable.

American behaviorist **B. F. Skinner** (1904-1990) devised a chamber, known as a **Skinner box**, to study the effects of various schedules of reinforcement on the behavior of small animals such as rats and pigeons. During **acquisition** or learning, each time a lever in the Skinner box was pressed, a food pellet was dispensed into a food dish. A speaker or light signal was also used to indicate conditions of reinforcement or extinction. In some studies, the grid floor was electrified, and the electric current could be turned off by pressing the lever. The speaker or lights signaled when the current would be turned on and in avoidance trials, the animal had a certain amount of time to press the lever to avoid the shock.

Shaping involves systematically reinforcing closer and closer approximations of the desired behavior. When a rat is first placed in the Skinner box, it doesn't know that pressing the lever will result in a food reward and may never press the lever on its own. Lever pressing can be conditioned through shaping — each step closer to the lever results in a food reward.

Discriminative stimuli serve as cues that indicate a response is likely to be reinforced. The light in the Skinner box can be a discriminative stimulus. When the light is on, lever pressing results in a food reward. When it is off, lever pressing is not reinforced. The animal will eventually learn to discriminate and to press the lever only when the light is on.

Punishment is also an operant conditioning technique. The goal of punishment is to decrease behavior. Punishment involves the presentation of an **aversive stimulus** or **undesirable consequence** after a behavior has occurred. Something negative can be added or something positive can be taken away. Receiving a ticket for speeding and being placed on house restriction are two examples of punishment.

Timing is very important for punishment to be effective — the sooner the punishment is delivered after the undesired behavior occurred, the better the learning. Even very short delays can reduce the effectiveness of punishment. Punishment must also be **severe** enough to eliminate the undesirable response.

Punishment may have undesirable **side effects.** Punishment often provides a **model of aggressive behavior,** and the person punished may learn that aggression is a method for solving problems. Punishment alone **does not teach appropriate behavior.** The person providing the punishment can become a **feared agent** to be avoided. Punishment can get out of hand and become **abusive.** Many behaviorists today suggest that punishment be avoided as a method used for conditioning. Instead, they recommend the use of extinction to weaken an inappropriate response and reinforcement to increase appropriate behaviors.

6.3 Observational Learning

Observational learning occurs when we learn new behaviors by watching others. This is sometimes called **social learning, vicarious conditioning,** or **modeling.**

Observational learning is guided by four processes:

Attention — Attention must be paid to the salient features of another's actions. Prestige or status of a model can influence whether another's actions are noticed.

Retention — Observed behaviors must be remembered in order to be carried out.

Reproduction of Action — We must be able to carry out the behavior that we observed.

Motivation — There must be some reason for carrying out the behavior. Observing someone being rewarded for a behavior increases the likelihood that the behavior will be performed.

Vicarious learning occurs when we learn the relationship between a response and its consequences by watching others. **Vicarious reinforcement** occurs when we observe the model receiving reinforcement. **Vicarious punishment** happens when we observe the model being punished for engaging in a behavior.

Edward Tolman (1886-1959) differentiated between learning and performance. **Latent learning** is learning that is not demonstrated at the time that it occurs. For instance, we may learn a behavior when we observe it, but never display the behavior. Thus, we may learn behavior but never perform it. Tolman maintained that behavior may not be demonstrated until it is motivating to do so.

The classic research on observational learning was conducted by **Albert Bandura** and his colleagues. This research included children watching and imitating an adult's aggressive behavior toward a **Bobo doll.** Bandura found that children learned the aggressive behavior even when the adult was not reinforced for this behavior. Later research indicated that children who watched an aggressive model being reinforced were much more aggressive in a similar situation than children who saw the model punished for the aggressive actions. Through his research, Bandura has demonstrated that both classical and operant conditioning can take place through observational learning — by observing another's conditioning.

CHAPTER 7

Human Memory

7.1 Encoding

Memory is the storing of information over time. **Encoding** is the process of placing information into memory. **Storage** is the process of retaining information in memory. Getting information out of memory is called **retrieval.**

You must pay attention to the information that you want to place or **encode** in your memory.

Fergus Craik and **Robert Lockhart** proposed three levels for encoding incoming information. They suggested that whether we remember information for a few seconds or a lifetime depends on how deeply we process the information. Information can be processed or encoded according to three different features:

Structural — Information is stored based on visual codes — what information "looks" like or its physical structure.

Phonemic — Information is stored based on acoustic codes — what it sounds like.

Semantic — Information is stored based on semantic codes — what it means. Most information appears to be stored in memory based semantic codes.

Levels of processing theory suggests that deeper levels of processing result in longer-lasting memory codes. The *deepest level* of processing appears to be semantic. Structural encoding is often a shallow level of processing and phonemic encoding is intermediate. **Allan Paivio's dual code theory** suggests that information is better remembered when it is represented in both semantic and visual codes because this allows for storage of both the word and image.

7.2 Storage

The **information processing theories** of memory emphasize how information flows through a series of separate memory stores. One prominent information processing model that was proposed by **Richard Atkinson** and **Richard Shiffrin** describes this flow of information through the **sensory memory** to **short-term memory** and finally to **long-term memory**. This model is described below and is presented in Figure 7.1.

7.2.1 Sensory Memory

Sensory memory (sometimes referred to as **sensory register**) holds sensory information for a brief period after the physical stimulus is no longer available. It holds an exact copy of the sensory stimulus for only a few seconds. More information enters our sensory memory than will reach our short-term memory. **George Sperling** developed a **partial report procedure** to measure this. Subjects were to report only some of the items from a visual display that they saw for a very short period of time (e.g., one tenth of a second). Sperling found that subjects were able to see more items than they could report and that subjects' memories of the visual display faded completely after about one second.

In general, sensory memory holds information just long enough to recognize and transfer it to short-term memory for further processing through a process called **selective perception** or **selective attention**. Selective perception/attention allows only specific information out of the many possible sensory messages bombarding us at any one time to enter into our conscious awareness. It is controlled by the focus of our attention and the set of expectancies we have prior to receiving the information.

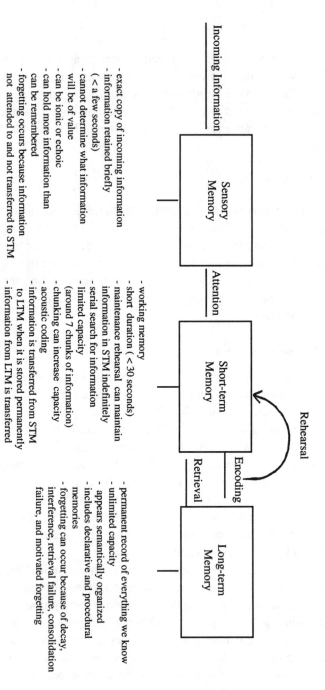

Incoming Information → Sensory Memory

Sensory Memory:
- exact copy of incoming information
- information retained briefly (< a few seconds)
- cannot determine what information will be of value
- can be ionic or echoic
- can hold more information than can be remembered
- forgetting occurs because information not attended to and not transferred to STM

Attention → Short-term Memory

Short-term Memory:
- working memory
- short duration (< 30 seconds)
- maintenance rehearsal can maintain information in STM indefinitely
- serial search for information
- limited capacity (around 7 chunks of information)
- chunking can increase capacity
- acoustic coding
- information is transferred from STM to LTM when it is stored permanently
- information from LTM is transferred into STM to be thought about
- forgetting can occur because of displacement and encoding failure

Rehearsal

Encoding / Retrieval → Long-term Memory

Long-term Memory:
- permanent record of everything we know
- unlimited capacity
- appears semantically organized
- includes declarative and procedural memories
- forgetting can occur because of decay, interference, retrieval failure, consolidation failure, and motivated forgetting

Figure 7.1: Model of Human Memory

66

Iconic sensory memories (or **icons**) are visual representations that last for only about one second in sensory memory. **Echoic sensory memories** (or **echoes**) are representations of sound sensory memories that may last for several seconds.

7.2.2 Short-Term Memory

Short-term memory (STM) is where conscious thinking and processing of information take place. Whatever you are thinking about right now is in your short-term memory.

Once information enters short-term or **"working memory,"** it usually remains there for only about 20 to 30 seconds because short-term memory is very sensitive to interruption or interference. **John Brown** and **Lloyd** and **Margaret Peterson** devised a method for measuring the duration of short-term memory. Subjects were presented with a stimulus and then asked to count backwards. This backward counting prevented active rehearsal of the previously presented stimulus. Brown and the Petersons found that by 20 seconds of backward counting, subjects could not remember the previously presented stimulus.

Unless the information is important and meaningful or is being actively **rehearsed** or repeated, it quickly leaves short-term memory and is "forgotten" when new information **displaces** it as we begin to think about something else. The material is forgotten because it was never learned. **Displacement** occurs, therefore, when new information enters short-term memory and pushes out existing material. For example, when you look up a number in a phone directory and dial it once, it is doubtful that you will "remember" the number at a later date. You held the number in your short-term memory while dialing. Within 20 seconds after dialing, however, the number was no longer consciously available and was "forgotten" as you began to think about something else.

In order to determine if certain information is in short-term memory, researchers have proposed that we could engage in a **parallel search** by examining all the information in short-term memory at once, or we could use a **serial search,** examining only one bit of information at a time. Research results indicate that the search process in short-term memory is serial.

Short-term memory is also limited in the amount of information it can hold. The average adult can hold between five to nine bits or **chunks** of information in short-term memory. **George Miller** proposed the **magical number seven, plus or minus two** as the capacity of short-term memory. The capacity of short-term memory can be increased by using bigger chunks of information or by what Miller referred to as **chunking.** Chunking involves organizing or grouping separate bits of information into larger units or chunks. For example, 5 8 1 2 7 8 6 3 could be chunked into 58 12 78 63. This transforms eight bits of information into four, thereby freeing up space in short-term memory.

Memory span is a measure of the capacity of short-term memory. It is the largest number of items that can be recalled perfectly from short-term memory after only one presentation and no time for study.

Although various types of memory codes can be used in short-term memory, it appears that **acoustic coding** dominates, especially for verbal information.

Information in short-term memory may be new information coming in from the sensory store or it may be old information coming in from long-term memory in order to be thought about and used.

7.2.3 Long-Term Memory

If *enough* repeated rehearsal or practice occurs, information may be transferred from short-term memory into long-term memory. **Long-term memory (LTM)** is our permanent storehouse of information. For instance, all the knowledge we have accumulated, all the skills we have learned, and all of our memories of past experiences are stored in our long-term memories. The more meaningful the information is, the more easily it can be stored in long-term memory. Some information is stored automatically from short-term memory into long-term memory without effort, usually because this information is highly meaningful. Most information, however, must be actively rehearsed in order to be transferred from short-term to long-term memory.

Unlike short-term memory, long-term memory appears to have unlimited storage capacity.

Information in long-term memory appears to be organized. Research has suggested that new facts are learned by fitting them into a network of pre-existing knowledge.

Propositional network theory suggests that we store meanings in propositional representations in long-term memory. A **proposition** is the smallest unit of information that makes sense. Each proposition is represented by an oval or circle, called a node, which is connected to the components of the proposition by arrows, called **links**. For instance, the proposition "dog" might be connected to the nodes "bark," "fur," and "four legs."

Research shows that there are at least two broad types of memory circuits in long-term memory:

Declarative Memory — "Fact" memories such as names, dates, events; related to thinking and problem solving; accessible to conscious awareness; can often be rapidly learned and rapidly forgotten; has been subdivided into **semantic memory** (store of factual information) and **episodic memory** (store of our personal or autobiographical experiences).

Procedural Memory — "Skill" memory such as remembering how to ride a bike, play a musical instrument, or eat with a fork; learned by repetition and practice and are hard to un-learn; often performed without conscious thought.

Some long-term memories seem to be visual. An extreme and rather rare example is **eidetic memory.** Eidetic memory is characterized by relatively long-lasting and detailed images of scenes that can be scanned as if they were physically present. They are rare in adults and occur more frequently during childhood.

Human memory is so complicated that long-term memory storage and retrieval do not appear to be limited to just one brain structure, although the exact process is not completely understood. When a memory is stored, communication at existing synapses is improved, and the structure of neuron parts near the synapse is changed. Research has shown that the **hippocampus** is somehow important in storing and retrieving memories, as are the **amygdala** and the **thalamus.** The hippocampus, amygdala, and thalamus all send nerve fibers to the **cerebral cortex,** and it is in the cortex that memories are probably stored.

Neurotransmitters are also important in memory. For example, patients with **Alzheimer's** disease have decreased amounts of the neurotransmitter **acetylcholine.** Drugs that interfere with acetylcholine neurotransmission impair memory. Drugs that increase its production sometimes improve memory.

7.2.4 Mnemonics

Mnemonics are strategies for remembering information. They work because they add meaning and context to hard-to-remember information. Several different mnemonics are described below:

Rehearsal — Repeating (or writing or reading) the information over and over. This is a primitive method for remembering. Other methods are more effective and efficient.

Elaboration — Thinking about how new material is connected or related to information already in long-term memory. This results in deeper levels of processing than simple rehearsal.

Method of Loci — Used to remember a list of items. Think of a familiar path or route and then visualize each item you have to remember at different locations along this path or route. For instance, you could visualize one item in your driveway, another in your garage, another at your door, etc.

Peg Word System — Can be used to remember a list of items in a set order. First, you memorize a list of words that will serve as "memory pegs" (such as "one is a bun," "two is a shoe") and then you create a visual image between the peg word and what you need to remember. For instance, if you need to remember the terms "dog and tree," you could visual a dog in between a hot dog bun and a Christmas tree that is decorated with old tennis shoes.

Organization — Reorganizing information into meaningful groupings. For instance, organizing spelling words for study based on identical prefixes.

SQ3R — Series of five steps that can be used to learn reading material. These steps include surveying, questioning, reading, reciting, and reviewing. This is also known as the

PQRST method: preview, question, read, self-recitation, and test.

Overlearning — Studying or practicing material beyond mastery — beyond the point where it can be repeated or carried out without error.

Metamemory — An effective way to improve one's memory is to become aware of it. Metamemory is our awareness of memory — how it works, its limitations, strategies for remembering, etc.

Spaced Practice — Short study sessions spread out over an extended period of time lead to better learning than does **massed practice** (one long learning or cramming session).

7.3 Retrieval

Retrieval involves bringing information from long-term memory to short-term memory so that it can be used or examined. Thus, whenever we remember anything, we are *retrieving* that memory from where it is stored. Retrieval is generally preceded by an internal process called **memory search.**

Retrieval cues help us gain access to a memory and can be any stimulus or bit of information that aids in the retrieval of information from long-term memory.

Two basic methods of measuring retrieval are:

Recall — Material must be remembered with few or no retrieval cues (e.g., essay tests).

Recognition — Task is loaded with retrieval cues; material must be remembered through identification of the correct response (e.g., multiple-choice tests).

Encoding specificity principle states that retrieval cues are more efficient when they are coded when the information is learned, and that retrieval success is most likely if the context at the time of retrieval approximates that during encoding. For instance, people remember more material when their psychological state or physical location are similar to what they were when the material was originally learned. This is referred to as **state dependent** and **locus de-**

71

pendent learning, respectively. According to **locus dependent learning** we should study or learn in a location or context that is as similar as possible to where we will be tested in order to maximize retrieval cues. The same is true of psychological state. If we are in a happy state when we learn material, we will be more likely to retrieve this information in the future if we are happy according to **state dependent learning.**

It is easier to retrieve beginning and ending items in a list and most difficult to remember the middle items. Recall being better for items at the beginning and end of a sequence is known as the **serial position effect.** Information at the beginning of a sequence is likely to be retrieved because it has already been placed in long-term memory. This is known as the **primacy effect.** Information at the end of the sequence is likely to still be in short-term memory and easily recalled, known as the **recency effect.** Middle items are least likely to be retrieved because they are neither in long-term memory nor in short-term memory.

The **tip-of-the-tongue experience** occurs when we are confident that we know information but cannot retrieve it. Even though the correct information cannot be recalled, it often can be recognized. This is because recognition tests provide retrieval cues about the needed information.

7.4 Forgetting

There are several theories that attempt to explain why forgetting occurs:

Decay Theory — If information in long-term memory is not used, it gradually fades over time until it is lost completely.

Interference Theory — Information in long-term memory is forgotten because other learning gets in the way of what needs to be remembered. Two types of interference have been described: **Proactive interference** occurs when old information in long-term memory interferes with remembering new information. **Retroactive interference** occurs when new memories interfere with remembering old memories.

Retrieval Failure — Not enough retrieval cues are available to prompt remembering.

Encoding Failure — The information was never learned; that is, the information never made it from short-term memory into long-term memory for permanent storage.

Consolidation Failure — Memories new to long-term memory take time to consolidate or be firmly implanted. Any disruption in the consolidation process can prevent a permanent memory from forming. Examples include a grand mal seizure, blow to the head, or anything that causes the loss of consciousness. **Retrograde amnesia** is the term used to describe a loss of memory for events occurring for periods of time *prior* to a brain injury. **Anterograde amnesia** is used to describe a loss of memory for events that occurred *after* a brain injury.

Motivated Forgetting — This occurs when disturbing, anxiety producing, or otherwise unpleasant memories are no longer consciously available because it would be disturbing to remember them. We tend to remember pleasant events better than unpleasant ones.

Hermann Ebbinghaus (1850-1909) was the first to plot a **forgetting curve**. He personally memorized lists of **nonsense syllables** (consonant-vowel-consonant trigrams, such as "wuf" and "rit") and later tested his own recall. He found that the longer the list of nonsense syllables, the more learning trials required. Ebbinghaus also found that most forgetting occurs immediately after learning, and then the rate of forgetting slows down considerably. This is what his forgetting curve documents. Ebbinghaus also measured **savings** or the finding that relearning the same material is quicker and easier the second time. The concept of savings is used as evidence that forgetting is never complete.

CHAPTER 8

Language and Thought

8.1 Major Properties of Spoken Language

Language and thinking are two abilities that make us uniquely human.

A spoken language requires the use of **signs** and **symbols** within a **grammar.** Grammar determines how the various signs and symbols are arranged and is a set of rules for combining the symbols or **words** into sentences. Language also allows us to use the signs and symbols within our grammar to create novel constructions.

Some characteristics of spoken language include:

Phonemes — The smallest unit of sound that affects the meaning of speech. The English language consists of 53 phonemes. By changing the beginning phoneme, the word "hat" comes "cat."

Morphemes — The smallest unit of language that has meaning. When speaking of more than one bat, we add the morpheme "s." Morphemes are often referred to as roots, stems, prefixes, and suffixes. Words are usually sequences of morphemes but one morpheme can constitute a whole word.

Semantics — The study of meaning in language.

Syntax — The set of rules that determine how words are combined to make phrases and sentences.

Phonetics — The study of how sounds are put together to make words.

Grammar — A broader term than syntax; it includes both syntax and phonetics.

Pragmatics — Includes the social aspects of language, including politeness, conversational interactions, and conversational rules.

Psycholinguistics — The study of the psychological mechanisms related to the acquisition and use of language.

Noam Chomsky distinguished between a sentence's **surface structure** (the words actually spoken) and its **deep structure** (its underlying meaning).

Two sentences, therefore, could have different surface structures but similar deep structures. An example would be, "The dog bit the boy" and "The boy was bitten by the dog." The surface structure of a sentence could also have more than one deep structure (e.g., "Visiting relatives can be boring."). When we hear a spoken sentence, we do not retain the surface structure, but instead transform it into its deep structure. Chomsky referred to this theory as **transformational grammar theory.**

Speech perception is guided by both bottom-up and top-down perception. **Bottom-up processing** in perception depends on the information from the senses at the most basic level, with sensory information flowing from this low level upward to the higher, more cognitive levels. For instance, the phoneme "c" in the word "cat" is perceived, in part, because our ears gather precise information about the characteristics of this sound. **Top-down processing** emphasizes the kind of information stored at the highest level of perception and includes concepts, knowledge, and prior knowledge. We are so skilled at top-down processing, for example, that we sometimes believe that we hear a missing phoneme. **Warren** and **Warren** found that subjects reported they heard the word "heel" in the following sentence where the * indicates a coughing sound: "It was found that the *eel was on the shoe." Subjects thought they heard the phoneme "h" even though the correct sound vibration never reached their ears. This is an example of top-down processing because prior knowledge and expectations influenced what subjects perceived they had heard.

8.2 Language Development

An outline of language development follows:

Cooing and Crying

↓

Babbling

↓

One-word Stage

↓

Two-word Stage

↓

Telegraphic Speech

↓

Verb Tenses, Meaning Modifiers, Pronouns, etc. Added

↓

Syntax Acquired

The first vocalizations that infants make include cooing and crying. At about four months of age, infants begin to **babble.** Their babblings are comprised of a repetition of syllables (e.g., "mamamama"). By six months of age, an infant is more likely to babble when an adult is talking to the infant. Babbling appears to be an innate ability because deaf infants who cannot hear usually babble.

Infants usually begin to understand several individual words that caregivers are saying by five to eight months of age. A child's first words are ordinarily spoken between 10 to 12 months of age. This is referred to as the **one-word stage** because they can usually only use one word at a time. The first words that children use tend to be concrete nouns and verbs. Children often underextend and overextend the meanings of their first words. **Underextension** occurs when a child only uses a word in a specific context (e.g., only says "duck" when in the bathtub with a toy duck but never refers to this toy by name when outside the bathtub). **Overextension** or **overgeneralization** occurs when a child uses a word to mean more than an adult speaker would. For instance, a child who calls *all* four-legged, furry animals (cats, dogs, etc.) "doggie" is overextending or overgeneralizing.

Some researchers have referred to children's one-word utterances as **holophrases** — that is, this one word could be interpreted to mean an entire phrase. For instance, a child points at an object and says "Cookie." This one-word could possibly mean, depending on context, "I want a cookie," "There is a cookie," or "Is that a cookie?"

Children from 18 to 20 months of age are in the **two-word stage** of language development because they are now making short, two-word sentences (e.g., "More milk," "Where ball?"). Their vocabulary is also expanding rapidly during this stage. They may learn several new words each day.

Telegraphic speech quickly follows the two-word stage and consists of sentences that do not contain any morphemes, conjunctions, prepositions, or any other **function words.** Telegraphic speech only contains the **content words** necessary to convey meaning, similar to a telegram (e.g., "Doggie kiss Jeff."). Children's first sentences follow the subject-verb-object sequence, and children often rely on this word order to make their meaning clear.

Eventually, children add verb endings, adjectives, auxiliary verbs, and morphemes to their utterances. Interestingly, initially children tend to use the correct verb tenses, even the exceptions (e.g., "went," "ran"). By age four or five, however, they are often using incorrect forms ("goed," "runned"). These errors seem to indicate that children are acquiring general rules about their language and for a period of time they overgeneralize these rules to the exceptions. Eventually children use the exceptions appropriately.

By age five, children have acquired most of the syntax of their native language.

When speaking to infants and older language-learning children, older children and adults typically use **motherese**. Motherese is speech that contains short sentences that are often repeated. This speech tends to consist of concrete nouns and active verbs. Pronouns, adjectives, conjunctions, and past tenses are usually absent. The sentences are enunciated clearly, often in a high-pitched voice. Many researchers believe that motherese helps children learn language.

An ongoing **nature vs. nurture** debate has been whether language is basically an innate, biological process or a learned phenomenon.

Many researchers hold the view that children are somehow biologically programmed to learn language. According to Chomsky, the **language acquisition device** gives children an *innate* ability to process speech and to understand both the fundamental relationships among words and the regularities of speech. Researchers have also proposed a **critical period** for language learning during childhood. If exposed to language during this critical period, language learning will take place. After the critical period has passed, however, language learning will be much more difficult.

B. F. Skinner and other learning theorists proposed that language learning takes place similar to other forms of learning described in Chapter 6. That is, parents selectively reinforce and shape babbling sounds into words. When parents speak to their children, children receive attention and often affection as well. Children then try to make these reinforcing word sounds themselves, i.e., try to imitate their parents, because it is rewarding for them to do so.

8.3 Elements of Thought

Thinking is defined as the manipulation of mental representations. **Cognition** includes the mental activities involved in the acquisition, storage, retrieval, and use of knowledge.

John Watson proposed that thinking is merely subvocal speech and is not a mental activity. He felt that we talk to ourselves *so quietly* that it is not apparent that we are doing so. Other researchers have confirmed that thinking is *not* subvocal speech. For instance, individuals who cannot speak can think.

8.3.1 Concepts

A basic element of thought is the notion of concepts. A **concept** is a label that represents a class or group of objects, people, or events that share common characteristics or qualities. We organize our thinking by using concepts, and concepts allow us to think about something new by relating it to a concept we already know.

Some concepts are well-defined, and each member of the concept has all of the defining properties; no nonmember does. These are sometimes referred to as **artificial concepts.** An example of an artificial concept would be "registered voters" — you either are or are not registered to vote.

Other concepts are not so clearly defined but are encountered in our everyday life. These **natural concepts** have no set of defining features but instead have characteristic features — members of this concept must have at least some of these characteristics. "Bird" is a natural concept. Birds range from chickens to sparrows to ostriches. **Prototypes** are objects or events that best represent a natural concept. A sparrow or robin would be considered prototypical birds by many individuals. New concepts are easier to learn if they are organized around a prototype.

8.3.2 Mental Imagery

Mental imagery refers to mental representations of things that are not physically present. Research has shown that imagery can play an important role in thinking. Some psychologists believe that thinking with mental images differs from thinking with words, just as pictures differ from sentences.

Some psychologists feel that we store mental images based on an **analog code** or a representation that closely resembles the physical object. Others argue that mental images are stored based on **propositions** or in terms of abstract descriptions and these descriptions are used to create an image.

Roger Shepard and **Jacqueline Metzler** reported evidence that supports the analog view of mental imagery. They found that it took subjects longer to rotate an object 180 degrees than to rotate it 20 degrees, just as it takes longer to rotate physical objects a greater distance. **Stephen Kosslyn** found that subjects make judgments about mental images in the same way that they make judgments about an actual picture. That is, it took them longer to make judgments about small mental images than about large ones. Forming large mental images took longer than forming small ones. These results also support the analog view.

Cognitive maps contain our mental images of what is where. They are mental representations of particular spatial arrangements. For instance, you probably have a cognitive or mental map of the United States, as well as one for your state, your town, your campus, your house, etc. Cognitive maps are not accurate copies of the environment but instead represent each individual's perspective. Researcher **E. C. Tolman** reported that even laboratory rats appear to form cognitive maps. As a result of experience in a maze, they seemed to develop a mental awareness of not only the physical space in the maze but also the elements within the space. The rats used their cognitive maps to locate food even when the usual path to the food was blocked.

8.3.3 Reasoning

Reasoning involves transforming information to reach a conclusion. It includes evaluating and generating arguments to reach a conclusion.

Inductive reasoning involves reasoning from the specific to the general. For example, drawing conclusions about all members of a category or concept based on only some of the members is inductive reasoning. **Deductive reasoning** is reasoning from the general to the specific. Making a prediction based on a theory involves deductive reasoning.

Logical reasoning includes mental procedures that yield valid conclusions. Formal tasks have been developed that measure logical reasoning. Two such tasks are **syllogisms** and **analogies.**

Syllogisms are arguments made up of two propositions, called **premises,** and a conclusion based on these premises. They require deductive reasoning.

For example, is the following reasoning valid?

"All cats are animals."
"All cats have four legs."
"Therefore, all animals have four legs." No, the reasoning is not valid. There are some animals which do not have four legs.

An **analogy** is a type of reasoning task that is always made up of four parts. The relationship between the first two parts is the same as the relationship between the last two. Analogies require inductive reasoning. For example:

"*Light* is to *dark* as *summer* is to _____." Light is the opposite of dark, therefore, summer is the opposite of winter.

8.4 Problem Solving

Problem solving is the mental activity used when we want to reach a certain goal that is not readily available.

Problem solving includes:
Understanding the problem.
Planning a solution.
Carrying out the solution.
Evaluating the results.

Problem representation or the way you think about a problem can make it easier or harder to solve. We can represent problems visually, verbally, with symbols (e.g., mathematically), or concretely with objects. A chart or **matrix** that represents all possible combinations of solutions could also be used to keep track of what solution has been and has not been tried.

Some problem solving strategies include:

Algorithms — Every possible solution is explored. Guarantees problem will be solved eventually, although can be time consuming.

Heuristics — "Rules of thumb" or shortcuts that help solve problems. They seem to offer the most reasonable approach to reaching the goal. However, there is no guarantee that a solution will be reached.

Subgoals or Means-ends Analysis — Intermediate steps for solving a problem. Part of the problem is solved with each subgoal. Often not obvious how to divide problem into subgoals.

Analogy — Solution to an earlier problem is used to help solve current problem. Often difficult to recognize similarity between problems, however.

Working Backwards — For a problem with a well-specified goal, you begin at the goal and work backwards. Worth considering when working forward has not been successful.

Expert Systems or Artificial Intelligence — Computer programs that solve specific problems. Most use algorithms.

Incubation — Putting the problem aside for a while and engaging in some other activity before returning to the problem.

Trial and Error — One solution after another is tried in no particular order until a solution is found. Can be very time consuming.

Some problem solving problems include:

Functional Fixedness — The inability to solve a problem because the function we assign to objects tends to remain fixed or stable. We tend to see objects only in terms of their customary functions.

Mental Set — Tendency to persist with old patterns for problem solving even when they are not successful.

Confirmation Bias — Tendency to confirm rather than refute a problem's hypothesis even when there is strong evidence that the hypothesis is wrong. Often tend to ignore information that is inconsistent with the hypothesis.

Creative problem solving involves coming up with a solution that is both unusual and useful. Creative thinking usually involves **divergent thinking** or thinking that produces many different correct answers to the same problem or question. Creating a sentence with the word "Springfield" would involve divergent thinking — there is no one specific correct response. A response to the question "What is the capital of Illinois?" would require **convergent thinking** — one correct answer is expected. Convergent thinking does not appear to be related to creativity. Although all creative thought is divergent, not all divergent thought is creative.

Tests (e.g., **Remote Associates Test**) have been developed that measure creativity. Almost all of these tests require divergent thinking. In general, these tests of creativity have not been good at predicting who will be creative in real-life problem solving situations. There is a modest correlation between creativity and intelligence. Highly creative people tend to have above average intelligence, but not always. Furthermore, having a high IQ does not necessarily mean that someone is creative.

8.5 Decision Making

Decision making requires you to make a choice about the likelihood of uncertain events. Although most of us try to be systematic and rational in making decisions, we do not always live up to these goals. We often lack clear rules about how to make the best decision. Similar to other cognitive tasks, decision making requires us to combine, manipulate, and transform our stored knowledge.

When we have no procedures to use in decision making, we tend to rely on heuristics that include availability, representativeness, and anchoring.

The **availability heuristic** involves judging the probability of an event by how easily examples of the event come to mind. This can lead to bad decision making when the probability of the mentally available events do not equal the actual probability of their occurrence. For instance, in deciding whether one should drive after consuming alcohol, one could decide that this would be a safe thing to do because nothing bad happened the two previous times driving occurred after alcohol consumption.

The **representativeness heuristic** occurs when you decide whether the sample you are judging matches the appropriate prototype. This is probably the most important decision making heuristic, and it usually leads to the correct choice. Decisions concerning diagnosing an illness are often based on the representativeness heuristic — that is, judging how similar the symptoms are to those of the specific disease.

An **anchoring heuristic** occurs when you estimate an event's probability of occurrence and then make adjustments to that estimate based on additional information. We tend, however, to make adjustments that are too small. For instance, you ran out of drinks at your last party. In deciding how many drinks to buy for this year's party, your estimate will probably be based on how many drinks you bought last time and how early into the party these drinks ran out.

The **additive model** is another method for decision making. It occurs when we rate the attributes of each alternative and then select the alternative that has the highest sum of ratings. Additive strategies for decision making are examples of compensatory models. **Compensatory models** allow attractive attributes to compensate for unattractive attributes. **Noncompensatory decision models** do not allow some attributes to compensate for others. One bad rating results in eliminating that alternative.

Decisions can also be made by **elimination of negative aspects** whereby less attractive alternatives are gradually eliminated. Alternatives are eliminated until there is only one that satisfies all the necessary criteria.

REA's **Problem Solvers**

The "PROBLEM SOLVERS" are comprehensive supplemental text-books designed to save time in finding solutions to problems. Each "PROBLEM SOLVER" is the first of its kind ever produced in its field. It is the product of a massive effort to illustrate almost any imaginable problem in exceptional depth, detail, and clarity. Each problem is worked out in detail with a step-by-step solution, and the problems are arranged in order of complexity from elementary to advanced. Each book is fully indexed for locating problems rapidly.

ACCOUNTING
ADVANCED CALCULUS
ALGEBRA & TRIGONOMETRY
AUTOMATIC CONTROL
   SYSTEMS/ROBOTICS
BIOLOGY
BUSINESS, ACCOUNTING, & FINANCE
CALCULUS
CHEMISTRY
COMPLEX VARIABLES
DIFFERENTIAL EQUATIONS
ECONOMICS
ELECTRICAL MACHINES
ELECTRIC CIRCUITS
ELECTROMAGNETICS
ELECTRONIC COMMUNICATIONS
ELECTRONICS
FINITE & DISCRETE MATH
FLUID MECHANICS/DYNAMICS
GENETICS
GEOMETRY
HEAT TRANSFER

LINEAR ALGEBRA
MACHINE DESIGN
MATHEMATICS for ENGINEERS
MECHANICS
NUMERICAL ANALYSIS
OPERATIONS RESEARCH
OPTICS
ORGANIC CHEMISTRY
PHYSICAL CHEMISTRY
PHYSICS
PRE-CALCULUS
PROBABILITY
PSYCHOLOGY
STATISTICS
STRENGTH OF MATERIALS &
   MECHANICS OF SOLIDS
TECHNICAL DESIGN GRAPHICS
THERMODYNAMICS
TOPOLOGY
TRANSPORT PHENOMENA
VECTOR ANALYSIS

If you would like more information about any of these books,
complete the coupon below and return it to us or visit your local bookstore.
